LEADERSHIP

GENERAL RICK HILLIER

LEADERSHIP

HarperCollinsPublishersLtd

Leadership
Copyright © 2010 by Rick Hillier.

Published by HarperCollins Publishers Ltd.

First Edition

HarperCollins books may be purchased for educational, business,
or sales promotional use through our Special Markets Department.

HarperCollins Publishers Ltd
2 Bloor Street East, 20th Floor
Toronto, Ontario, Canada
M4W 1A8

www.harpercollins.ca

Library and Archives Canada Cataloguing in Publication
Hillier, Rick, 1955–
Leadership / Rick Hillier.

ISBN 978-1-55468-493-9

1. Leadership. I. Title.
HD57.7.H545 2010   658.4'092   C2010-903049-4

Printed and bound in the United States
RRD 9 8 7 6 5 4 3 2 1

This book is dedicated to those thousands of leaders whom I got to appreciate each day—to those from the most junior to the most senior in the CF, to their families, across the departments of government in Ottawa and to those leaders in the civilian community who continue to be such incredible supporters of the men and women in the CF. I particularly pay tribute to those who get that leadership is all about people and that remembering that fact means you won't go far wrong.

CONTENTS

INTRODUCTION

I was in downtown Toronto in the early afternoon of 20 January 2009, walking among the towers that are the headquarters of our major businesses and corporations, while in Washington, DC, President Barack Obama was being inaugurated. I found it most interesting to watch people in their cubicles and offices in those towers, glued to TV or computer screens, watching the inauguration as though hypnotized. And, somewhat unexpectedly given our perception of how many Canadians view the United States, they all seemed to be watching with what I believed to be envy. They wanted Canada to share the vision, clear thinking and strategic approach that Obama was articulating for our great southern neighbour. They wanted visible leadership.

Later that afternoon I contrasted the scene from Washington—one of hope, excitement, vision and daring—to the kind of junior kindergarten antics that we see each afternoon during

Question Period in the House of Commons in Ottawa. I know that Canadians want something better than that dismal display. They want true leadership.

People want to be able to be a part of something greater than themselves. Nobody wants to live and die alone. They want to improve the society they live in. They want their communities to be better, so they join chambers of commerce, Rotary Clubs, Lions Clubs, hockey associations, artistic groups and volunteer fire brigades. Most people understand intuitively that working together gives them enormous potential and allows them to accomplish more than working separately. And they look for leadership to help those individuals achieve more together as a group than they could alone. That is to say, we actively seek people who can bring the leadership necessary to help us become more, and achieve more.

Within those communities, clubs, associations, hobby groups, churches and schools, individuals quite naturally gravitate to those who can bring people with different backgrounds, beliefs and characters together and start them working toward one goal. These leaders are visible in communities across the country. They provide the unifying force, the leadership, to help individuals come together with a common purpose and do more. That's incredibly positive for the communities where we live, for our country and, indeed, for the entire world.

People will move from one leader to another to satisfy their desire to contribute or to make a greater impact—to be part of something powerful. People will change churches, schools, club associations and even their careers to find what they seek. Even informal leaders have to work hard, and deliver, in order to keep people following them. Since in most cases those informal leaders are also trying to do more, to make a greater impact by leading than by acting alone, they have a vested interest in being effective as a leader, to get more done.

Someone steps forward with a vision, however simple, with a plan to do something or with an idea that inspires all the rest to follow. The result is that kids become more responsible, and eventually become better Canadians as adults, and we are rewarded with safer communities, less crime, reduced poverty and much, much more. None of it is possible without leadership.

But that is in good times. In tough times, people seek leadership for entirely different reasons, and that is when leadership matters even more. When something goes wrong—a natural disaster, a company closing its doors and doing away with jobs that are a community's lifeblood—people get scared. And when they are scared, they look for comfort from one another, seek psychological security and hope and, most important, reach for answers to find a way out of the chaos and insecurity that surrounds them. They first seek guidance within their circles of friends and colleagues, those they know or at least know of. They are looking for a leader to step forward. They want someone who understands their fear, can see through the fog to what the future can bring, can articulate the best way to proceed (even if he or she doesn't always have the perfect solution), understands the risks, and, with personal courage and by leading through example, can motivate frightened people. In tough times, people search for that lead dog to take the pack on the journey.

There is perhaps no better example of a leader in recent history than that of Winston Churchill during the Second World

War. In the darkest days of the British Empire, when the future of that great democracy was at stake, this incredible man stepped forward. With a stubbornness that resonated with the British and the other free peoples of the world, a blunt pragmatism that came across as the truth no matter how unpalatable, and an ability to understand his people's overwhelming fear during those difficult days and address that fear directly through his words and actions, Churchill changed history. With his famous words, "I have nothing to offer but blood, toil, tears and sweat," he appealed to those spilling their blood in the air, working against all odds to stem the vicious Nazi tide, shedding tears for lost loved ones and sweating profusely during the bitter fighting in the North African desert. His defiant stance in itself mobilized the free world to resist in a way that few leaders, if any, have ever done. He inspired, as the formal leader, in this time of grave danger, and people followed. In the end, after the danger was over but before the end of the war, the British people kicked him out of office, although he was later, in peacetime, re-elected as prime minister. Leaders have to continue to work hard to bring what people who are following them want, or else those followers will find a leader who can.

Closer to home, in April and May 1997, the Red River Flood, quickly dubbed the "flood of the century" by media and government, inundated large parts of southern Manitoba and the city of Winnipeg, threatening those who lived within the flood plain. Record snowfalls the winter before, combined with exceptionally rapid spring thaws and heavy rains, turned the normally placid, forty-metre-wide Red River into a raging torrent forty kilometres wide. Homes were flooded, farms were isolated, bridges were destroyed and government structures were pushed beyond their capability. The Canadian Forces, in the largest deployment to a natural disaster to that date, were called on to help out.

My brigade out of Petawawa, Ontario, was en route at exactly that moment to the Maritimes for a spring training exercise. We rapidly reversed course and headed west. Within forty-eight hours, a train of hundreds of earth-moving, tracked vehicles, along with four thousand soldiers and my team of senior officers and non-commissioned officers, made their way to Winnipeg. It immediately became evident to us, first and foremost, that the civilian organizations already in place were not prepared to cope with disaster of any scale, but especially not with something this big. All those federal, provincial and municipal governments and agencies were well prepared for good times, but not for bad. No one was in obvious command; committees of dozens were the norm, and decisions, if made at all, were unclear and often revoked as quickly as they were communicated. At first, the Canadian Forces was not particularly welcome. We were seen as just one more organization thrust into a situation that already had more than enough—until one civil engineer read out the latest reports that a wall of water, estimated at thirty metres high, was moving into Manitoba from the south. That amount of water blew away everyone's most dire predictions. The engineer quietly and calmly told the civic and provincial officials in the room that none of their hydrographic tables could offer any indication of what would occur next.

The change was palpable. The military became the most sought-after people in the province, because we had prepared leaders, the ability to make detailed and effective plans and a tendency to act where others talked. People wanted someone to take charge. It didn't matter whether they were the homeowners surrounded by floodwaters—the dykes they had built in danger of collapsing—Winnipeg city councillors who wanted to help safeguard their constituents or bureaucrats in the provincial government, resistant until then to any outside help, people were all now looking for leadership.

Our role in the Red River Flood was the seed that led to the regrowth—a rejuvenation, really—of the Canadian Forces and its relationship with Canadians. Bob Meating, commanding the brigade out of Edmonton and on the ground before me, provided much of that leadership and helped me and my team get engaged and into the thick of things in a hurry. The most precious commodity in that time of stress and fear was leadership.

Something similar happened in January 1998, less than eight months later, when the "ice storm of the century" struck eastern Ontario and Quebec. Power was out and telecommunications had been interrupted by the weight of accumulated ice that caused the huge steel hydro towers and telephone poles to come crashing down. Roads were blocked by fallen wires, and in a matter of hours, life was dramatically altered for thousands of Canadians. Again, my brigade, just two hours up the road from Ottawa, was called to action. We arrived to find a situation terribly similar to what we had seen in Winnipeg.

Those living in the fifty-three Ontario municipalities that declared states of emergency needed support not only to stop the situation from getting worse but to return things to normal; they needed to have hope that things would be all right in the end. What was again obvious to me was that they wanted someone, anyone, to bring all the awesome power of a country together to achieve that. The City of Ottawa, under the newly elected chair of Ottawa-Carleton Region, Bob Chiarelli, provided much of that leadership for the biggest city affected by the storm. But outside Ottawa, leadership was largely missing. When the Canadian Forces showed up, prepared, energetic, experienced and ready to act, the tens of thousands of rural residents looked to us for leadership, and our people, our leaders, shone. Men and women like Walter Natynczyk (now Chief of the Defence Staff), Stu Beare, Hilary Jaeger (now the highest ranking female in the Canadian Forces) and Mike Jorgensen stepped up. So enthusiastically did they throw themselves into their temporarily assumed roles that we had to almost drag them out two weeks later in order to allow civil authorities to once again take charge. Again, in our own country, with our own citizens, the most precious characteristics during those troubled times were those that called out "leader."

Internationally, examples abound of leadership in both good times and bad. Lieutenant-Colonel Ian Hope led his battle group of about a thousand men and women throughout a series of intense operations against Taliban insurgents over a long spring and summer in 2006. In their attempts to help lift the yoke of oppression from the good people living in southern Afghanistan, Ian and his troops were in constant combat operations. They sustained losses, grieving the deaths of battle buddies and long-time friends, and learned a lifetime of lessons in that six-month deployment.

It all culminated on 3 August, in heavy fighting in Panjwaii District, west of Kandahar City in Kandahar province, strategically the most important of provinces in the country. In the brutal heat of the Afghan summer, with temperatures in the fifties Celsius, taking casualties and with numerous wounded soldiers, Ian was called upon to lead like never before. His battle group had lost momentum and gone to ground under severe Taliban fire in a part of the country ideal for ambush, defence and running away to fight another day (particularly if you knew the ground as well as the Taliban fighters did). Heavy concentrations of those well-prepared fighters had dug in and were delivering a withering amount of fire, so much that the scene was eerily reminiscent of First World War battles. The storm of bullets and grenades raining down on them came as a complete shock to young Canadians, raised in a country of privilege and security. Despite all the scenarios their commanders had predicted and the situations for which they had trained as soldiers, this was almost inconceivable.

However well they had been trained, nobody, from the commander to the most junior soldier, was prepared for such fire. That they were able to not only survive this test but ultimately triumph is the greatest compliment to our soldiers and to their ability to turn their training, initiative, imagination and innate abilities into actions leading to overwhelming success.

In his forward command post very near the fighting—the bodies of several long-time friends lying next to him waiting to be recovered, and numerous battle and heat prostration casualties seeking the shade of the command post—Ian Hope recognized that the eyes of nearly a thousand soldiers were upon him. He felt the weight of command and responsibility as never before in his more than twenty years of service. As he went, they would go. With his regimental sergeant-major, Wayne Northrup, Ian moved to the most forward section under fire and got those soldiers moving, fire from one group of four support-ing the movement of the second group and then vice versa. His actions that day started a palpable change, a movement that sec-tion by section, then platoon by platoon and finally company by company, started the battle group forward to achieve what he wanted them to do. Men and women whose overwhelming instincts when they were under murderous fire were to hide, go to ground, disappear, instead got up and, in the face of machine-gun and rocket propelled–grenade fire, did their job. One leader, a superb Canadian, led the way by personal example to a sig-nificant success in a situation that could easily have resulted in a devastating defeat with long-term, extremely negative strategic implications.

Long after those events in 2006, a Taliban commander paid his foes the ultimate compliment. In a 2010 interview, Commander Mullah Haji Mohammed held forth with the usual Taliban fundamentalist rhetoric, providing predictable answers to predictable questions. But when asked whether foreign sol-diers were all cowards, his answer was surprising.

"Yes," he responded, again predictably, "they are all cowards, and without their machines, their planes, vehicles and technol-ogy, they would not last more than a month." He paused and then added: "On the other hand, you do have a few brave invading sol-diers; from all the invading countries, the Canadian soldiers are the most brave."

Ian had been formally appointed to a leadership role, but the vast majority of the leaders who change communities, whether local, regional, societal or worldly, do not hold any formal posi-tion of leadership. They are the men and women who stepped forward to help improve things during good times. They are often the ones who intuitively understand that a community can achieve more with leadership than without it, and when they see that a void exists, they step forward to fill it. In tough times, even if they don't step forward, they are often propelled or pushed to the front of the pack because of those same attributes.

History abounds with examples of successful leadership. In India, Mahatma Gandhi changed a society that was tearing itself to pieces, community pitted against community. In the process he changed the world with a simple vision of the dignity of mankind, a vision exemplified in his daily life and his constant, powerful message delivered through both words and actions.

The diminutive Mother Teresa, the personification of dignity and courage, also changed the world for the better, not because she was politically powerful but because her simple actions and efforts to serve others spoke so loudly. Martin Luther King, whose words, delivered in a deep, melodious and hypnotic voice, moved millions to look inside themselves, shaped our society and changed our understanding of basic human rights in a way that perhaps nobody in history had before him. John F. Kennedy, with his challenge to Americans and the rest of the world to "ask not what your country can do for you but what you can do for your country," helped us all understand what leadership was and how important leaders are. Mahatma Gandhi, Mother Teresa and Martin Luther King weren't presidents, CEOs or generals, but they had such a powerful and positive effect that there is hardly a living human being who would not recognize them for what, and who, they were. Most important, they are remembered for the leadership they brought, in their own unique ways, to change the world.

A person does not have to be on the national or international stage, hold a formal leadership role or be looked to by millions in order to have a powerful effect. All around you, among your family, friends, colleagues, acquaintances and neighbours, there are leaders. You too will find the opportunity to lead, and while you take those opportunities, you are gaining experience and growing confident in your ability to be a leader, whether it be in business, in a profession or in politics.

In Canada, the Army, Navy and Air Cadet Leagues of Canada are probably our best Canadian programs for producing responsible Canadian citizens among young boys and girls aged twelve to nineteen. As a commanding officer of the Royal Canadian Dragoons Army Cadet Corps in Lahr, West Germany, in 1983 and 1984, I have a soft spot for this powerful nationwide citizenship program. It is regrettable that in the 1970s, at the height of a flush of anti-militarism in Canada, we removed it from school programs.

The cadet program emphasizes leadership. It teaches and puts into practice the same principles that major corporate, military and international leaders learn at Harvard University, in graduate programs across our own country, in military schools or even from the school of hard knocks. The thirteen-year-old girl thinking about what she wants to have her section of six other cadets achieve during a weekend training event at a local park works through the same strategizing and planning that other leaders must, then communicates her plan and encourages or inspires others with her guidance and supervision to implement it. Our youngest son, Steven, now fully engaged in his adult life, swears to its importance in his initial success in the private sector. Confidence, public speaking, mental organization, practical leadership, planning under stress and knowing how to handle deviances from the plan are attributes and skills not taught, let alone practised, in many places, but the cadet league is one place where they are.

My point is simple. If you are young, get involved. Volunteer and get out front to organize, contribute and get things done. If possible, join the cadets. In leadership, practice makes perfect, just like with most other activities in life, so get that practice. Become part of the chamber of commerce, get involved in a charitable foundation, help organize food drives for the needy, coordinate support to improve the lives of the elderly, start a cleanup of your neighbourhood—do anything, but just start, and keep thinking of the ways you can become a leader and make a difference. Be a leader in relatively small ways and you will become a better, more polished leader in bigger ways.

If you are older and at a critical point in your career, with greater challenges available through leadership appointments, make yourself competitive. Take on voluntary activities, look for the opportunity to run a project and get that practical experience—it's worth its weight in gold.

———

There is great debate as to whether leadership can be taught, and therefore learned, or if some people are just born with innate leadership abilities, as part of their DNA. I have straightforward opinions on this based on both experience and observation.

Clearly, you can learn to be a manager, overseeing daily process and procedures in an organization where people are slotted into comfortable roles. These tasks are quantifiable and so can be regurgitated in the form of lesson plans, seminar discussions, practical exercises and interactions with people. It's telling how many corporate and governmental-organization assessments of the people who become executives—leaders—are exclusively management focused: how well do they handle the files in the inbox, or interview people, or organize their time? But there is almost no assessment of their leadership skills. This is in part because many management activities can be easily measured and in part because so much of what we call leadership is subjective and therefore difficult, if not impossible, to measure. It is difficult to put leadership qualities on a chart or graph, though we know intuitively that some people inspire us and others do not. It is much easier to judge managers based on a written job description that defines their duties. Sadly, this creates in our society an almost complete focus on management, with very little attention being paid to leadership, despite marketing that touts executive MBA programs as creating "leaders." Make no mistake: they are in fact management programs.

My view of leadership is that it is a combination of art and science that, when practised, gets people to do more as a group than they thought humanly possible. And, I believe, it can be taught. At the very least, budding leaders will always have the opportunity to learn from the mistakes of others. We can and must teach people to become leaders. I'm not certain that leaders such as Churchill, Ghandi and King can ever be developed through a leadership program, but if people are born with at least some of the right DNA, they can learn enough to effect enormous change.

Experience has led me to believe that people generally fit into three categories in terms of leadership or leadership potential. One group, roughly 15 percent of people, have the characteristics and skills to be very good, perhaps even great, leaders, no matter what their training. They will make the right decisions intuitively, inspire people naturally and with a little good luck achieve incredible things. And they always seem to make their own good luck.

Another category, comprising another 15 percent, have no ability to lead, no matter how much is invested in their education, training, experience or mentoring. Most of those in this category understand this, whether consciously or not, and are comfortable doing something that doesn't involve a leadership role.

The final category, the remaining 70 percent—the hump in the bell curve—is the group that determines success or failure. With education, good training, honest assessments, solid examples and worthwhile mentoring, all of these people can become leaders of a sort: the ones who propel an organization forward in good times, those who lead well in routine times, and those who are quietly at work until disaster strikes and then show what they're made of. Given the opportunity, and with support, anyone can achieve his or her full leadership potential, both for personal benefit and for the good of the company, organization or community.

I was in this last category, part of the 70 percent majority. Opportunities came to me because I paid attention and learned leadership skills. You can do the same.

I learned much of what I know from poor leaders, including the fact that actions speak loudly and that it's important to be present, to be seen by your subordinates. For example, early in my military career I watched one of my commanders get up in front of us, a group of soldiers, on his last day with us and apologize for spending too much time in his office and not enough with the front-line troops. I decided then and there that I would never put myself in a position to have to make that speech. My core beliefs are to never disrespect anyone and to recognize the efforts of others; this means always showing my appreciation, helping them to focus and trying to inspire them.

One of the greatest requirements of a leader is the ability to communicate. I encourage everyone to become strong public speakers. Some people, however, communicate best in other ways: through actions, in writing, with a joke, or through drawing, sketching or models. What do I mean by models? Let me give you an example. On one occasion during training in a foggy, wet, cold and desolate area of New Brunswick, I had to give orders for a battle group attack (involving close to a thousand men and women and some seventy-five vehicles). In the middle of the night, I had to lay out a rock-and-stick model that would show a group of fatigued people how to conduct a complex and dangerous attack on a well-prepared, well-equipped and alert enemy.

That was difficult enough. But imagine how much more difficult it was with incoming artillery fire (simulated, of course) that forced me and my team to jump under cover every five or ten minutes. As well, radio silence was imposed on us to maintain operational security, making it a challenge to mount our seventy-five vehicles and move them over fifteen kilometres in the foggy darkness.

But my crude little model worked—an example of the possibilities and strengths of models, pictures and simple schematics. Because of that model, all the members of the team, even though fatigued and cold, could visualize the mission, ground, possible enemy actions and their roles in the operation. The operation went smoothly, again thanks in large part to the model. Use any and all of your strengths to meet the need, and don't be mesmerized by what works for someone else. You can learn those things and by doing so learn to be the leader you wish to become. Art and science are not inseparable.

In their writing on command and leadership, researchers Carol McCann and Ross Pigeau identify three styles of leadership: autocratic, transactional and charismatic. Autocratic leaders impose their authority, their plans and their ideas on their followers without acknowledging their followers' ideas. Transactional leaders share their planning and ideas with their followers. Charismatic leaders indoctrinate followers with their ideas and plans. It's this last kind of leader that I have always tried to focus on becoming. In my view, three characteristics mark this type of leader. First is the long-term approach to the role; that is, having a vision for achieving much more as a team than either the leader or followers could as individuals. This has the effect of raising everyone above and beyond daily drudgery and bringing people together in sharing the leader's plan willingly. The second characteristic is setting a strong personal example in everything he or she does. The third is a never-ending focus on the people who follow. Combined, these three characteristics eventually bring everyone in the team together to share the leader's intentions, plans for the future and goals.

One of the great abilities of charismatic leaders, particularly evident when they set examples in carrying out tasks, is that they understand the difference between the theory behind doing something and the practical aspects of actually accomplishing it. They know what they can get done by simply using common sense. In other words, they are not just book smart, they're also street smart. As Yogi Berra so famously said, "In theory there is no difference between theory and practice. In practice there is." Charismatic leaders recognize this early and act accordingly.

These three characteristics—vision, personal example and focus on people—form what I call the holy trinity of leadership. These characteristics set you up for success, first by combining the focus you as a leader must have on your goals and objectives with the gifts you have been given, and then through the actions you take. Almost every one of the successful leaders I've watched or worked for excelled because of this combination of vision, personal example and focus. Keep it in mind every day: focus on your vision of what you want you and your team to achieve and inspire your people to get it done, set a flawless personal example that you want others to emulate, and concentrate on those who want to be led to ensure they want to be led by you.

If there were only one thing I could take away from all my years and experience, it would be this: leadership is about people. Remember that, and you have the foundation that will set you on your way to becoming successful and having enormous potential to conquer future challenges. Forget that focus and you have taken the first step toward failure.

It's equally clear to me what leadership is not about: organizational charts, corporate structures, process, or the latest management theory or technology. Although all of these things can complement you as a leader (sometimes, sadly, they do just the opposite), they are not the focal point that you as a leader should spend your time on. Focus on people.

PART 1

NEVER FORGET—
IT'S ALL ABOUT PEOPLE

PUT PEOPLE FIRST

It's people who make you, and your company, organization or community, successful or not, in good times and bad. Everyone wants to be successful. I often ask people, "Have you actually ever met anybody who wanted to go to work on a given day and fail?" The answer is inevitably no, and yet the way we conduct ourselves and develop relationships with those who work for us often suggests the opposite: we expect failure and therefore shape our efforts to defend, rather than shaping them to win.

That's why, as I said earlier, men and women get involved in many things in life: they want to be successful. They coach kids judo, soccer and hockey teams; organize dance groups; lead boys and girls clubs; organize Scotch-tasting clubs; fundraise for local food banks; and through their leadership and involvement help make their communities better places to live.

Your job as a leader—as *their* leader—is to focus those impulses, to get them to think long term and to adopt your vision for the company or organization. You may even find, if you do that well, that people will help you improve your vision and sharpen its focus. You have to motivate and inspire people, enable them to do their jobs as well as they can, sustain them in their endeavours, recognize them for their productivity and, eventually, say farewell to them with dignity and respect as they leave for their just rewards in new challenges or retirement.

As a leader you want to inspire your people to be so engaged and committed, to have accomplished so much that even when they are ninety-five years old, sitting in a rocking chair on the back porch, they will look back on their time under your leadership with the satisfaction of accomplishment and contribution, and a feeling that they have made a difference. What they will remember most is how you made them feel as they did their work and focused on their job. Only then can your job as a leader be considered complete.

None of the people around you will be supermen or superwomen. Indeed, I've never met a superhero, even among the incredible men and women I commanded in my more than thirty-five years in the Canadian Forces, and I've concluded that superheroes really don't exist. As journalist Christie Blatchford once told me very forcefully, as only she can, heroes in our society are those who have had the label slapped on them by others. The men and women who look to you for leadership are not going to be heroes. Despite my admiration and love for men and women in uniform, I knew they were ordinary people, but that they accomplished superhuman tasks because of their commitment and dedication to their organization, their belief in the goodness of our country and their faith and belief in their leaders (including, from time to time, me).

One such Canadian is Conrad Cowan, based at Canadian Forces Base, Comox, British Columbia, in central Vancouver Island. Conrad is a member of an exclusive fraternity in the Canadian military: he's one of only about 140 or so men and women who are SAR Techs (search and rescue technicians). (Women have just recently completed the selection process necessary to be in this gruelling profession, and their tiny numbers will undoubtedly increase.) SAR Techs, with their air and ground support crews, spring into action in the worst of times; that is, when Canadians and, occasionally, those of other nationalities are in danger of losing their lives. Many times, the threats to these people arise because of the dangerous nature of their livelihoods—they are fishers on the high seas whose boats burn or sink, Native hunters in the North who get trapped on ice that has broken free from the land, pilots who encounter unexpected weather or mechanical problems that cause their planes to crash. Equal in numbers, though, are those in danger of dying because of stupidity: recreational fishers who are drunk, mountain climbers who don't prepare, hikers who have not paid attention to their travels or the time of day. SAR Techs try to rescue them all, no questions asked.

In an average year, our SAR Techs participate in rescue operations involving more than eight thousand Canadians who are in trouble, often in danger of losing their lives, in a wide variety of environments and situations. More than one thousand of those Canadians are probably alive each year only because of the heroic actions of Conrad, his fellow SAR Techs, their aircraft crews and the leadership and sustainment teams that support them.

Conrad and the other members on a Cormorant search and rescue helicopter team were involved in an intriguing rescue that came to my attention. The rescue began when the team was alerted that a climber in the Rockies, a man climbing alone (a basic no-no), had slipped and fallen into a crevice. By the time the climber had reached someone on his cell phone, his life was already slipping away—clinging to a ledge in a deep crevice with night and freezing temperatures to combat, he was severely injured and going into shock. His chances of survival were slim.

Conrad and his ready crew launched in their Cormorant from Comox, just as the last glimmer of daylight faded. They flew the helicopter, something roughly the size of a Greyhound bus with a rotor on top, into the mountains and in the dark winter night found the deep chasm into which the climber had fallen. The pilot held the massive aircraft about fifty feet from the cliff face where the climber was, about one thousand feet off the ground, and tried to hold it steady in the strong mountain cross-winds—hellish conditions even for talented search and rescue crews. Conrad was lowered into the crevice on a thin wire hoist to search for the injured climber. They lowered Conrad down and then down some more, until more than three hundred feet of wire had been let out and the crew in the aircraft had lost sight of him. With only intermittent communication with Conrad, who wore a helmet with a walkie-talkie, the pilot, who is also the mission commander on these kinds of rescues, was ready to abort the mission. After all, with the chances of a successful rescue so low, there wasn't much sense risking the lives of five people to not save one.

It was at that critical moment that Conrad spotted the injured climber on the narrow ledge and, using the pendulum motion of the cable, managed to swing himself over to the man, then grab him and snap him into the harness. The two of them were hoisted up to the aircraft, and so the injured, shocked and badly chilled man was brought back from the edge of the precipice and death.

I got to know Conrad when I was Chief of the Defence Staff. Just twenty-eight years old at the time of the rescue, he is dedicated and accomplished; he wears several decorations for bravery on his uniform, like so many of the SAR Techs. When he came to Rideau Hall to meet Governor General Michaëlle Jean during a Canadian Forces heroes ball, I had the opportunity to ask him what his thoughts were during those risky hours.

"Conrad," I said, "when you were on that mission, more than three hundred feet below the aircraft, on a thin wire, deep in a dark and freezing crevice, at enormous risk yourself, what were you thinking?" I was not sure what I expected to hear from him, probably something like "This is what we do" or "Our training prepares us for this" or "The equipment permits us to succeed," but I was surprised by his response.

"Sir," Conrad said, "all I could think was, 'When my wife hears about this, she's going to kill me!'"

When I finished laughing, my first thought was what a touching testimonial this was to the ordinariness of these incredibly accomplished people. Then I thought about how this ordinary man, a great Canadian, did such astonishing things because of his belief in his mission and his dedication and commitment to the greater things in life. As a leader, you want to inspire and motivate all those whom you lead to be Conrad Cowans: dedicated, committed and armed with an insurmountable will to succeed, even though they are just ordinary men and women. That's how leaders change the world.

It wasn't only Conrad, however, who cemented in me this belief that as a leader you are all about people. I saw it everywhere I went. Visiting soldiers recently returned from Afghanistan—those who had been wounded, sometimes severely—always brought the people part to the fore. There they were, often lying in bed with needles and tubes jutting from every part of their bodies, and all of them, every one, came through as the good men and women they were, human to the core.

Corporal Shaun Fevens, from Halifax, Nova Scotia, was in the US Army's Regional Medical Center in Landstuhl, Germany, when I first saw him. He had been wounded badly in a terrible attack on Easter Sunday 2007; six of his fellow soldiers in the same vehicle were killed. Shaun, who had been partially out of the rear hatch doing his job as "air sentry," that is, observing to the rear and side for threats, was sucked down into the vehicle by the explosion and then blown, along with the armoured rear ramp (weighing at least a ton), away from the vehicle. He regained consciousness quickly and directed fellow soldiers to tie off his badly destroyed legs to prevent blood and fluid loss. Shaun was not about to die—not after surviving an attack like that—because of a lack of application of training. When I saw him about forty-eight hours after the attack, he was as composed and calm as anyone I'd ever met. His concern was for the well-being of his mom and his fiancée, Lana. They were obviously worried about him, but his concern certainly was not for himself. His thoughts were on what challenge and opportunity he would have in the future as a soldier. In fact, Shaun's first words to me were: "Is there still a place in the army for me?" ("Absolutely," I responded.) His second question then was about when he could finish his mission in Afghanistan (a question I often heard from wounded soldiers), and his third had to do with whether he could still become an officer and realize his dream of more, and different, challenges as a leader.

Everything about meeting Shaun and visiting with him brought home to me the fact that he was human, with emotions, with concerns, and with dreams that he wanted to realize. He was not a process, not something that could be described as a resource (how I detest the term "human resources") and certainly not a machine. There had to be a human connection for him to perform at his very best, and as a person he needed the respect due him. He and the thousands of others like him are the very essence of our country. As I once said when speaking as army commander back in 2003, "Our best weapons don't roll on wheels or get propelled by tracks; they travel on combat boots because they are human beings." This perspective must remain foremost in our work.

People like Shaun must be our focus as leaders. They need us to be equally real to them, that is, to be human, in order to be successful. Seeing Shaun's concern for his mom and his fiancée, I told him that I was returning to Canada and that I would phone each immediately upon arrival to tell them that I had seen him, touched him and spoken with him, and that he was going to be good to go. And I did just that, though only to find that Shaun had already phoned them to tell them I would be calling. Am I ever glad I did not miss that duty.

My wife, Joyce, and I have been constantly in touch with Shaun and Lana (now husband and wife). We introduced them to Team Canada at the IIHF World Championships in Halifax, held their new baby boy and, compliments of Toronto-Dominion Bank, spent almost a week with them in Charleston, South Carolina, where both of them impressed hundreds of TD leaders and their families as incredible human beings and Canadians who help make our country strong. The standing ovation they received after I introduced them was heartwarming and sent chills down my spine at the same time. At the Atlantic Canada Top 50 CEO Awards dinner on 12 May 2010, I had the great pleasure of introducing Officer-Cadet Fevens to the attendees: Shaun was continuing with his plan for life.

Lieutenant Simon Mailloux, a platoon commander with the Royal 22nd Regiment, the Van Doos, out of Valcartier, Quebec, made a strong impression on me as well. While doing his job leading his soldiers in Afghanistan, Simon was wounded in an attack that killed several of his soldiers. His vehicle was destroyed by an IED (improvised explosive device) and, in the fire resulting from the explosion, grenades and ammunition in the vehicle began to detonate. All of this with Simon lying in the middle of the wreckage, his leg terribly wounded—a leg he would later lose below the knee in surgery. When I saw him at the hospital in Quebec City, he too asked me if there was still a place for him, as a leader, in the army, and how soon he could return to Afghanistan and finish his mission. He also wanted to know what I, as his commander and leader, could tell him about his future.

As I visited with him, the humanity of this great Canadian almost overwhelmed me. Clearly distraught and emotional because he had been unable to prevent the deaths of his soldiers, missing his right leg below the knee, with months of rehabilitation in front of him, he was not going to be content with process, emails, risk management or anything else that did not recognize him as a person with dreams and goals he wanted to fulfill, with a contribution he wanted to make and with emotional baggage that he would carry. He was a person—flesh and blood—and needed to be assured that that was how I saw him.

Simon reminded me yet again where my, and our, focus had to be, and I continue to be inspired by him. Yes, there was a place for him in the army; yes, we needed him as a leader; and yes, he could return to Afghanistan as a leader as soon as he was ready. That he has since done so is powerful testimony to what you can accomplish if you remember that those you work with are human also. One of the great moments of my last hour as Chief of the Defence Staff was inspecting, with the Governor General and my incoming replacement, General Walter Natynczyk, the right flank of the parade, which consisted of heroes from across the breadth of the Canadian Forces, including Simon. The emotion of seeing him, as well as Paul Franklin, Lincoln and Laurie Dinning, Warrant Officer Hooper and so many other heroes, was very moving.

These people who had been through some of the very worst days of their lives together remembered most fondly the days that made them feel hope for the future. Each remembered how others made them feel. The medics in Kandahar—men and women from across our country and from around the world— were remembered by each of our wounded not because of their amazing medical technology or the well-oiled machine that is our hospital and casualty evacuation infrastructure—though both were certainly important to their survival and recovery— but because of the compassion with which they cared for their patients.

I made it a point to visit our hospital in Kandahar every time I was in that country, just so I could speak with, and thank, those men and women who did their life-saving work with such compassion. On one visit I saw an Afghan father, unable to speak English, who had lost two sons in a landmine explosion and whose little girl was injured. Already traumatized by the ongoing encounter with a foreign culture (and particularly one in which women were leaders), he watched with awe and some trepidation as the men and women treated his daughter, the only child he had left. Although she was probably seven or eight years old, she looked to be about four because of malnutrition. She had lost a leg and a hand, was blinded in both eyes and had shrapnel wounds (forty-seven, if I recall correctly) over her entire body. Watching one of our nurses just sit and stroke her hand spoke to me of the power that comes when you enable people to be themselves and meet their aspirations. As Chief of the Defence Staff, I was this young nurse's leader. My job was to ensure she was trained well and shared my vision of the mission in Afghanistan and how we were to carry it out, to put her in that hospital, then let her do the rest. As a leader, that was one instance where I succeeded beyond my wildest dreams.

I was touched by every story I heard of the accomplishments of the men and women of the Canadian Forces. My job as their leader was to enable them, to give them the motivation, the plan and the tools to achieve the amazing things they so often did. They were, first and foremost, good people. They were also people with awesome skill sets. And, finally, they were men and women working within an organization that empowered them to do what we wanted them to do in pursuit of success, with world-class tools and technology to support them. That was why those medical professionals were so capable and compassionate. Almost every Canadian soldier I talked to who went through the US military's Landstuhl Regional Medical Center was equally effusive in their praise of the men and women there (almost all Americans). The vast majority returning home were just as generous in their praise of the men and women of our own medical system here in Canada. I must admit, it did make me wonder why we beat up on our healthcare system so much of the time. All of these medical professionals, after years of training and preparation, were remembered for exactly the same reason—the way they made people feel. Those soldiers were treated as people, with compassion, humour and love.

31

CHAPTER 2

BUILD YOUR NETWORK IN GROUPS OF EIGHT

Building for success in groups of eight is a lesson from the First and Second World Wars that we have relearned in the Canadian military since becoming engaged in combat operations in Afghanistan, but the lesson is equally applicable to any company or organization. I became focused on it after a discussion with Lieutenant-Colonel Ian Hope and others in his leadership team during a visit to his deployed battle group in Taliban-infested country around Kandahar City in the summer of 2006. Ian talked at length about the natural warrior, the one who carried the unit and ensured the mission would be a success no matter what the odds. Ian told me that when facing machine-gun fire and grenade explosions, normal men and women seek shelter, but the natural warrior (which he called *Homo furens*, Latin for "fighting man"—though there are certainly women in combat operations now too) keeps going. Natural warriors are rare, and it was exceptional to find more than a couple in any grouping.

What we had found, however, was that with good selection, training, mentoring and experience, any group of eight people will almost always give you at least two natural warriors. Any fewer than eight and the chances are much lower that it will include two natural fighters. The important thing was that two natural warriors in a group of eight, what the army called a rifle section, were all it took to make that team of eight soldiers successful. They would be the ones who set the example for the other six to follow; they would be the ones who, when normal instincts screamed to seek cover by going to ground, would get up from shelter and, bringing fire to bear with a coolness that amazed those who saw it, fight through an enemy ambush or defensive position, even if it resulted in their own injury or death.

In any company, the natural warriors are those who under stress find the solution to complex problems and make a company's product successful. They are the ones who have found their niche in life; what they want to do fits perfectly with the company's vision and complements the leader's work completely.

It's a leader's business to find, identify and empower these natural warriors. They are not always clearly identifiable; in fact, natural warriors are very often invisible and may even be seen as the opposite of what they really are. For example, a significant percentage of those in the Canadian Forces who stepped up under fire were those who were constantly getting into trouble in garrison or during training. They performed at their best when the demands on them were so high that few others could meet them. These natural warriors usually are not the ones who identify with routines and procedures, and risk aversion is unnatural to them. As the army discovered during the intense fighting in Afghanistan, often natural warriors show themselves only when stress is at its highest and they, with their teams, find themselves at the edge of a precipice. On one side is success, and on the other, dramatic, perhaps even tragic, failure, with equal chances for either eventuality.

A group of eight in each critical area of your company has the statistical probability, if you've picked the right people and developed and trained them properly, of having at least two natural warriors who will lead you and the others to success. And that's just as true whether your natural warriors are salespeople or lawyers or mechanics. They are the people who get the job done when things are at their most difficult.

In the army, three sections of eight soldiers each are grouped into a platoon, plus a leader. Three of those platoons are put together, with supporting weapons detachments, into a company; three companies, plus supporting troops, form a battalion. When the battalion has its full complement of soldiers, its strength is almost a thousand people. But the core that will make that battalion successful consists of the natural warriors, two of them in each eight-soldier section, six in a platoon, eighteen in a company and somewhere around sixty in a battalion. That's what will guarantee success: sixty "employees" out of roughly a thousand. Finding, identifying where and when you can, empowering and supporting those sixty (or whatever the number) natural warriors is the core business for you as leader.

Amazing to me too is how even small changes can improve the potential for success. If for some reason your personnel selection process or the way you develop your people doesn't work well, and if your recruiting of talented individuals isn't what it should be, you might end up with only one natural warrior in your teams of eight. Or even—a major catastrophe—no natural leaders at all. We found that one natural leader, by him- or herself, could not always inspire the other seven members of the team. That section, when you needed it most, would go to ground and not get up. Worse, when an initial group of eight fails, the failure can be contagious, spreading to the platoon of thirty soldiers (including the platoon headquarters), the company of about one hundred and twenty and, eventually, the entire battalion. Thus, one or two individuals in a group approaching a thousand can be the difference between success and failure.

The same principle applies beyond the military. The bank branch manager, for example, who keeps a positive attitude in the midst of an economic crisis that sends tremors through customers' finances and shakes their faith in the bank could be your natural warrior. Or it could be the technician who continues to serve your customers, dealing with their problems and keeping them happy in the middle of a power outage or Internet crash. In times of crisis, the natural warriors are the ones who keep doing the critical jobs that keep your business or organization going despite the crises all around them.

The potential for a small number of people to have a positive effect is great. A grouping, whether a platoon or a company or some other, that has a "shine" on it will attract people who want to be there. When that's complemented by development of these people and good leadership, you can end up with three or four natural warriors in each small team of eight. And when that happens, you can change the world.

Imagine, for instance, that in your section you have a person like Ernest "Smokey" Smith. Born in Vancouver, Smokey received the Victoria Cross, the highest award for valour in the British Empire. He was just twenty-nine years old when, in Italy during the winter of 1944, almost all of his section was killed or wounded during a night battle over a small river crossing. Smokey single-handedly knocked out two German tanks and fought off more than thirty troops attacking his position. The contagious heroism of soldiers like Smokey has a positive effect on other sections, platoons, companies and even the entire battle group around them. Only two or so people out of a thousand can make that difference, and if you can attract this "cream of the crop" to you, the implication can be enormously positive. You, in your company, can change the world with a similar approach, blowing away the competition, building a legacy and achieving all that you ever dreamed of doing.

You can't count on having a Victoria Cross–winner working for you, but if you can spot the natural warriors in your organization, train them properly and put them to work in the small teams of eight that work so well for the military, they will repay the investment you put into them many times over. These are the people who produce for you when you really need them to.

ALWAYS SHOW RESPECT

People are the basic building blocks of everything you do as a leader and the most basic element of leadership is to treat people with respect. Never demean, insult or belittle your people, even in jest. Instead, build up their pride by showing them that each and every one of them is a respected, mature and responsible adult. That respect will be returned to you many times over, especially if your people feel that they are part of a powerful team.

My guidance to our soldiers when I led them—often as they went into dangerous places with the expectation of facing violence—was that there was never an acceptable reason to disrespect another human being. Even if the enemy was shooting at you, there was no reason to disrespect them, no reason to rob them of their dignity, even up to the point at which you killed them. Treat people like the mature, responsible men and women they are unless they prove, by their actions, that they are not. The vast majority will not disappoint you.

After I took command of 2 Canadian Mechanized Brigade Group in Petawawa on 14 July 1996, I spent the next several weeks visiting each of the units that made up this team of more than four thousand men and women. Each day with a different unit was generally a repeat of the day before, and started with physical fitness training—I thought there was no sense preaching about the necessity of being fit without demonstrating that I trained to be fit myself. I then had a meeting with the officers over coffee, followed by a walk through of the unit lines, where I took the time to talk with the soldiers who were preparing for their next mission, maintaining equipment or training. I met with all the non-commissioned officers after lunch to talk with them and then, to close the day, met and talked with the entire unit, sometimes seven or eight hundred people.

I said the same thing to each unit: "This is all about people. We work hard, our work is based on values, we apply common sense and we respect each other." This summed up what I wanted to represent. No matter the rank or appointment, seniority or ability, each Canadian in the brigade was a responsible, mature adult and would be treated as such unless his or her actions indicated he or she should be treated otherwise. There were precious few in that four thousand whose actions told our leadership team that they were not deserving of respect as individuals. Conveying that respect was often so simple to accomplish: having eye contact, acknowledging them as individuals, shaking hands as equals, accepting their input and opinions as part of developing our way forward and helping them feel that they were valuable members of the team, with a commitment to the success that relied on them.

The response was phenomenal. Several timely actions, small but important, allowed me to make the point visibly. The first opportunity to start to shape the way our leadership team would operate and how we would focus on people came in the first days of my appointment as commander, when it became overwhelmingly obvious that this formation—which had been conducting operations in the Balkans, preparing for other potential operations around the world and in Canada, and continuing to train hard at home—had lost some sense of balance between work and family. Units, hundreds of soldiers strong, trained Monday to Thursday for missions that involved peacekeeping or combat operations and then, from Friday to Sunday, trained for others, such as domestic response to natural disasters in Canada. The soldiers were tired. They saw no light at the end of a tunnel of repetitive training. Their families were also tired. The constant training, combined with the impact of the Somalia hearings, budget cuts and all the other characteristics of this "decade of darkness," made for devastatingly low morale. Cynicism was rampant, and most wearing the uniform couldn't wait to move on to another career.

So I made a decision. "Saturdays and Sundays," I said, "are family time, and we will not train then. We will not deploy to other areas on those days, or return." (Often, if we travelled to Meaford or Barrie, units started movements on Saturday or Sunday to be in place to start training on Monday.) "If there is such an urgent requirement as to demand that we work on those days, the commanding officer of that unit can justify it to me, personally, before the event." That simple change, augmented by new leaders in various appointments in the units at every level, had an astonishing impact. The soldiers could actually be seen smiling occasionally, and spouses tapped me on the shoulder at the grocery store just to say thanks. They had never seen so much of their partners, and their children had never seen so much of their fathers or mothers, and that one issue became a defining point for the serving men and women and their families in 2 Canadian Mechanized Brigade Group: they were important, they were respected and they would be supported and looked after. It was obvious from the leadership team's actions.

Another action, also done early in my days as brigade commander, had even more impact, further emphasizing to those incredible young Canadians who I was trying to lead that they were highly valued and would be accorded the respect they had earned. We were dealing with devastating federal budget cuts that affected everything we did but, in particular, our care for the base and its infrastructure. We did not have any money to hire people to cut the grass, trim the trees, clean up the roads or maintain the many buildings on Canadian Forces Base Petawawa. Our garrison quickly became rather seedy looking. It didn't take long for orders from my superior headquarters to arrive telling us to clean it up, and if we didn't have the money to hire people to do it, to use soldiers.

To me, those were fighting words. After spending every waking hour convincing the men and women serving in the brigade and supporting us from other units that they were professionals, called upon to do demanding and in some cases doctoral-level work at home or around the world because they were the only ones who could do it, and that our nation's very existence depended on them and their efforts, I was not about to ask them to mow the lawn. The last thing I wanted to do was now say to them, "You are the world's best, most professional soldiers, but since we can't afford to pay a few people the minimum wage to cut grass and clean up—you, the most highly trained snipers in the world; you, the engineers who set the world standard in explosives handling; and you, the finest tank and fighting vehicle crews in NATO—your job now is to cut the grass."

It took a while, but we won the fight. I refused to have our soldiers fill a hole left by budget cuts. Once news of the issue got out, the soldiers in the brigade realized that their leaders looked upon them as valuable members of a team and were willing to fight to make sure they were treated that way. The credibility and mutual respect earned so early in my command tour made the next two years probably the most enjoyable of my life.

Mutual respect allows an interaction between you and those in your charge. These people will invest their all for their team and to further its goals. Without that respect, their bodies will still show up for work every day, but mentally they just won't be there. Non-commissioned officers (the corporals, sergeants and warrant officers who are the backbone of every military) in the army of the 1970s and 1980s had a cynical saying for enthusiastic young officers like me: "You get my body for free, but you really have to work to get my mind." The power of the team you lead is not getting the bodies of people, or their minds; it's getting both. That's what you need to be successful, but that's also what you have to work so hard to get. Respect is the baseline for it.

As a leader, you can avoid pitfalls simply by keeping your focus on your people. Do what it takes to spend time with them, build up your relationship with them, openly discuss where you and they, as a group, are going and what it is you are trying to achieve. Don't be one of those managers who rule through email, avoid discussion, disappear into their offices in tough times and frame responses to hard questions in what is politically correct language instead of speaking clearly and honestly. As I was repeatedly told during my military career, spend time with the troops and you have the basics already set to show them the respect they deserve. The benefits in return will be powerful.

MAKE VALUES AND PRINCIPLES YOUR FOUNDATION

There have been many leaders throughout history who, at first blush, might be described as capable, confident and perhaps even great. People followed them without question and would do anything for them; they accomplished much while they were leading and their legacy remained long after they were gone. But looking more closely, it's clear that these people were not leaders, or certainly not the kind of leaders we would want to lead us or that we would want to be ourselves.

These so-called leaders lacked values. General Ratko Mladic was commander of the VRS, the Bosnian Serb Army, during the fighting in the Balkans in the 1990s; now he's a wanted war criminal. Revered by his men, audacious in his tactics, gregarious to all (except his enemies, or the weak and vulnerable civilians unlucky enough to get in his way) and brave as any of his soldiers, he could accomplish wonders. His men wanted to follow him. Yet this man lacked even the most basic of human values, killing, brutalizing, torturing and ethnically cleansing in the most terrible fashion any who opposed him.

Values are the basis of any strong organization. Groups with strong values share common goals. Individuals within the group who trust each other have confidence that the others in the group will perform at the level they expect them to. And they are confident that, as a result of their performance, they as individuals and the group itself will have credibility—that they will be successful.

Much study has been done on how to focus values in the achievement of goals through principles. I believe in values and principles. I have read much about them, and this combined with my experience as a leader has given me a certain perspective.

I believe that values must be taught to future leaders and to all those who want to belong to and become a contributing part of any group of people. Strong values make us different from those without strong values. Lieutenant-Colonel Ian Hope, commanding the Princess Patricia's Canadian Light Infantry battle group in southern Afghanistan in 2006, used to tell his men and women that the only difference between them and everyone else in southwest Asia carrying a gun was their professionalism and their values. Those values were diverse, deep and important to all, whether they knew it or not. These values included loyalty, respect, dignity and courage, both moral and physical. I agree with Ian. Values separate us from that which we do not want to be.

Although we all like to think that it is not necessary to teach values—that we have families, friends, schools, churches, boys and girls clubs, communities and employers to do this—it has been my experience that many in our society are missing a fundamental understanding of what values are, and their meaning. We must make an investment—of resources, people and time—to cement values. Ignorance may not be a defence under the law; nevertheless, if someone does something through ignorance, it can be costly. By asserting a value structure, you are again taking steps to build a team, a common and shared intent and the confidence of each team member.

It is never too late for people to learn values. Some experts assert that character traits are cemented by age four, others says it is by age eight, and still others say it can be at any age. I've read, for instance, that by the time someone is twenty years old, his or her values are set in stone. Bull. People can learn, and if they can learn, they can change, and that includes understanding values and their importance, and acting on them. I feel comfortable taking this stance, since another of my beliefs is that as a leader you must challenge the experts. I'm as expert in people as anyone.

When teaching values, you should also teach the standards of behaviour that correspond to an individual and define what is acceptable. You, through teaching, set a clear standard for people to follow and live up to in your organization. Even the strongest of people weaken from time to time for one reason or another, and having a clearly defined standard for the organization helps those morally stronger but occasionally tempted people to resist doing something unethical. For instance, if your employees see you and their co-workers always doing the right thing, they will be far less likely to fudge their expense accounts or do something equally unethical. It also helps those whose value systems are less than robust understand the enormous implications of their actions and therefore helps them resist the temptation to ignore the values they should be embracing. Educate those in your charge as to the values that are most important, define the absolute minimum standard for each value (yes, let people know that the expectation is more than the minimum), look people in the eye when articulating your expectations and enforce your guidelines scrupulously.

Select carefully the values that you believe should shape your team—after all, they should be practical and applicable to your organization, to you and your employees—and communicate them clearly, in person. And before you do that, seek out as much advice as you can, from whatever sources are at your disposal. There are many potential sources of advice on which values you should be emphasizing to your team, and almost all of them are important in their time and place, but in total they can be bewildering, contradictory and even downright dangerous. Ensure too that your organization's training and education component is paying particular attention to what you are saying. You need to be certain that what you are saying the values are—those values you have carefully selected to emphasize in your organization—and what the trainers and educators understand these values to be are the same thing. Values such as resoluteness, integrity, respect, compassion, inclusiveness and loyalty can mean different things to different people and in different situations. The best way to ensure that you and your team are on the same page is to hold the kind of frank discussions that are a healthy part of the teaching and training process.

Having poorly focused or misunderstood values can be as dangerous as having no values at all. We faced just such a challenge in the Canadian Forces in the 1990s. We had managed, over decades during which loyalty was taught and instilled in our air, land and sea combat units, to create somewhat conflicting demands when loyalty to the unit and to Canada pulled in different directions. This is because we had not taught our units loyalty to the Canadian Forces, and through that, loyalty to our country, assuming it to be self-evident. When soldiers were loyal to their unit, that loyalty was often in conflict with their loyalty to the Canadian Forces and to Canada. For decades, the regiment came first, above all else. Squealing on others in the unit or airing a regiment's dirty laundry for others to see was viewed as disloyal, even if rules and regulations of the Canadian Forces and Canada had been broken. In many ways, our combat units had created an impression among impressionable young men and women that their loyalty was first and foremost—perhaps even exclusively—to the unit, and if the country deteriorated and the Canadian Forces disappeared, as long as the regiment's dignity remained, they had done their job. The Somalia Inquiry exposed our faults. But, as in all learning experiences, our pain meant that others didn't have to go through the trauma that we did.

Part of establishing the confidence of your people and having them aspire to common values is recognizing what a potent threat situational ethics, or situational values, can be. I do not believe it can be anything but harmful to have values that shift, or disappear altogether, depending on the situation. I don't believe that everything's fine if an employee exhibits the right values at work, meeting the standards and demands of others, then at home rips off his insurance company by lying to the customer service rep to reduce his costs. In my belief, one begs trouble for the other. The otherwise honest, loyal and respectful individual who steals only on the weekends will invariably bring that lack of values to work. There is no getting away from it. So beware situational ethics.

As I've said, actions speak loudly. People cannot see values, ethics or principles per se, but they can and will see your actions. Your behaviour articulates your values more clearly than any words you speak. It's important that what you say and what you do match up. If you value loyalty up and down the organization, don't criticize your leader if you expect not to be criticized by those who call you their leader. Equally, if courage is a central value, you cannot penalize those who exhibit it in their defence of new initiatives, ideas and work. They will see your words as empty and meaningless. If that value of courage is basic and you require everybody in your team to defend their work, but you yourself are found wanting when it comes time to defend an unpopular or controversial item, it will have negative implications.

Lastly, if you teach and practise the values you want to see embodied in your organization, it can bring people who believe in them even closer together as an integrated team. That will allow your people to work more efficiently toward a common goal. Principles allow most people to put values into play in the areas most commonly understood and respected. In the Canadian Forces, as we started making many significant, long overdue changes, values proved to be of supreme importance to us, particularly when it came to articulating the Chief of the Defence

Staff's Guiding Principles. First, I said, our loyalty is to Canada, but our first loyalties within the military are to the Canadian Forces. "Be proud," I said, "to be a sailor, soldier, airman or air-woman, but not so proud as to be stupid, not so blindly loyal to your environment or unit that you cannot effectively make decisions for the betterment of all, but loyal so you can work within one hyper-efficient team that can accomplish much more for Canada."

This was important because my belief was that with the Canadian Forces lacking a vision, the component parts of that organization—the army, navy and air force—had gone into survival mode. The air force saw its salvation in working with NORAD or NATO in the high-altitude world of jet combat at forty thousand feet, the navy saw its salvation as working with the US Navy's huge aircraft carrier task forces and the army saw its future in high-intensity fights similar to those of the Second World War or the first Gulf War. No one within these three components was really interested in or even capable of working with the other elements of the Canadian Forces, which was ultimately to the great detriment of our country. We had to change; we had to work together.

My principles continued along that line, and I stressed that commanders had responsibility, authority and accountability while commanding missions, and their staff supported them. For too long we had allowed large staffs to overwhelm commanders and eventually undermine their authority. The principles were guiding lights for doing things based on values, and both these principles and values were enabling us to achieve common goals. Used intelligently, they are incredibly valuable.

CHAPTER 5

THE IMPORTANCE OF BEING YOURSELF

Being a leader is tough enough. But when you try to maintain a facade—pretending to be someone or something you are not, and presenting a false front to the world—it makes your job as a leader exponentially more difficult. Always be yourself; it makes your life so much easier and your performance as a leader that much better. This came clearly to my attention when I was in command of several formations of troops. One of those formations, made up of hundreds of young men and women, had all the reason in the world to be the best organization in the world. The troops had a clear and exciting mission, and their equipment, although it wasn't the best in the world, was at least appropriate to the task. The training that each individual in that unit received was superb. This training was why most of them had responded to the recruiting advertisements to "fight with the Canadian Forces." They should have been the happiest and most contented soldiers in the world.

Sadly, they were not. The unit was clearly disgruntled and unhappy, and it showed in various ways: relatively high rates of absenteeism, a lack of esprit de corps in competitive sporting events, numerous disciplinary actions and a lower retention rate than usual. Other formations, with much less support and fewer advantages, were by far happier and more enthusiastic, and those formations got the benefit of the complete commitment of their soldiers. I started spending a lot of time with the unit that was obviously so unhappy, and one day the cause became clear to me.

Standing with the commanders early one morning, waiting for the troops to arrive and fall into formation for physical training, we were passed by many of the soldiers—non-commissioned officers and young officers—most of whom joked with me or at least said good morning. One of the burdens that I carried in life came to the fore, as most of the jokes were about the dismal performance of the Toronto Maple Leafs the previous season and the unlikeliness that they would be better in the next. What was remarkable, however, in the repartee, the jokes and the good-natured digs between the senior commander, me, and even very young and junior soldiers and officers, was that not one word was directed to their immediate commander, who was standing next to me. Looking at the last officer to pass by, he said, "I used to be that way, smokin' and jokin' with the boys, when I was a junior officer and leader, but as soon as I became a commander that all changed. Now, it's all serious business and no time for jokes or making light of things."

I was, for once, speechless and it took a few seconds for me to respond. "Why," I said him, "do you think you were promoted through a variety of ranks, given additional challenges at each one and finally, now, given the challenges of senior command?

Because of the characteristics you exhibited, demonstrated and matured at each of those different levels. You were promoted to your present rank and given this challenge because of the kind of person you were and how you related to people. The last thing in the world we wanted you to do was change in such a fundamental manner." I no longer had the same confidence in that leader who had abandoned what made him so successful at each preceding level.

You have to be who you are. If you're a hard person, nobody will be fooled by a soft, people-friendly approach, and they will keep you at a distance. Similarly, if you're a people person who suddenly becomes a dictator, you will not be comfortable in your own skin, and those in your charge will notice immediately. Being someone you are not will lead only to a loss of credibility. This does not mean that you, if you're a soft people person, won't have to make tough decisions or have them made for you. But do an honest assessment of your traits, and balance the people around you to achieve that same balance in the team.

In the Canadian Forces, and particularly in the navy, we worked hard to achieve the best possible balance in the command teams, pairing a commander who was tough and hard with a deputy commander who was more people-friendly, and vice versa. Everybody in a leadership team came from one end of the spectrum or the other. A group made up of the same type of personalities was a recipe for disaster for both the leaders and their team.

If your forte is executing a task or running an operation, find someone whose strength is planning, to complement your abilities. Conversely, if planning is your strength, get a good operator to run things for you and be secure enough to let him or her do it with your guidance and support. Above all, be yourself.

Being compassionate is critical in building and maintaining the confidence and credibility of those you lead. If you try to not show emotion or wear a mask to cover your humanity, it will be as obvious to those around you as it will be to you. You are human, with muscles and bones that can fail, emotions that can get the better of you, aspirations that can inspire you to greater heights and even fears that can, on occasion, keep you awake at night. There's no sense pretending that none of these things affects you.

Masking your identity when a leader can take many forms. One thing some leaders do to hide their weakness is refuse to take time off. Despite the tempo of work and the intensity and stress of the job, they consider themselves too valuable to take a vacation. Some even believe that they don't need a vacation. Everybody else around them, however, sees things differently, and they are the ones who carry the burden of a worn-out leader who can't see that he or she needs a rest. Leaders like this are a burden to those in their charge and rapidly lose those people's respect. Don't become this kind of leader. The next time you attend a funeral, think about the person in the coffin. The stories you'll hear at the funeral won't be about how much time he or she spent in the office, that's for sure.

CHAPTER 6

DON'T FOCUS ON ORGANIZATION AND PROCESS

I have nothing against systems, or process, at all. In fact, I am fully supportive of the great impact they can have in helping a leader and team achieve their goals. They become part of what I call "doing the routine things routinely" so that you have time and energy to manage the opportunities or crises. What I am adamantly against, however, is process, particularly overwhelming process, put in place as a substitute for vision. Excessive processes don't inspire people to excel, and they don't work as a replacement for a strategic approach or for building a network of people.

I'm a firm believer, for instance, in the system Ron Joyce built to make Tim Hortons the part of Canadian culture that it is today. His system guaranteed the structure, service, uniforms, quality and efficiency of service in each franchise across the nation, throughout the northern United States, and in

Kandahar, Afghanistan. Ron did this by building his network of people and then, with an unequivocal and well-understood vision, coupled with strategy and focus, enabled those people he had recruited and led, with the system and technology necessary, to succeed beyond anyone's wildest dreams. He got the people part right first, and that allowed the system to be an enabler, rather than an obstacle.

It is easy to think of those qualities that don't make for a good leader, and easy to describe what a leader can't focus on if she or he wants to be successful. There are those in charge, for example, who spend inordinate amounts of their time, energy and resources creating the perfect organization (which usually exists only on paper—that is, in theory, as opposed to in practice), charting out who reports to whom, what the parallel relationships are, how each part of the organization should interact and where they themselves are in the organization. They seem to forget that it all changes once you insert people into the mix and that while all the work and time is being invested in finding that perfect organizational diagram, people have already found the practical ways to get things done. As a leader, you're far better off copying these practical methods than spending your time visualizing perfection. Think of it as a new housing subdivision: if you get the major routes in place and in the right spots, it's almost preferable to wait a year before putting in the sidewalks and walkways; after a year, you simply build them where people have already been walking, which will be obvious by the paths worn in the grass.

Some leaders waste their energy on the appointments within their organizations, designating ranks and titles for the clarification of all. Still others, often those who are insecure in their domain, focus all their zeal, energy and time on the process to be followed—what route a file must follow and what checks it must receive before it can proceed to the next level in a never-ending series of levels. It is a long time before anything actually gets decided, let alone done. For the insecure, this process is a good thing because it can be measured, tabulated, assessed and changed. Charts can be filled out, PowerPoint presentations built and briefings and reports completed. They become a full life's work in themselves.

Such managers try to cater to, foresee and deal with each perceived mistake by a person whose mind they have not brought onside. Because they have not inspired and focused people with a vision and by thinking long, they attempt to control and guide the actions, on a short-term basis, of those who work for them with comprehensive process that reduces risk by making the chance of individual error, whether inadvertent or deliberate, rare. Each deviation from the process that brings these managers a reprimand or public censure tightens the process itself and reduces the risk of that supposedly negative thing ever occurring again. They attempt to mitigate risk to their organization or mission by being so comprehensively detailed in what they do that they end up increasing the risk despite themselves. In fact, as my friend Walt Natynczyk said of these types of managers, they become "self-licking ice cream cones" where process becomes product and nothing much actually gets done because it is too risky. That, of course, is the greatest risk of all. There are always more options to be considered, more questions to be asked and answered and, invariably, another reason to say no.

In their misguided attempts to reduce risk, those transactional managers—and they are plentiful—have increased the risk to complete; nothing will be done and failure will be the result.

Travelling extensively in Europe during the outbreak of the foot-and-mouth disease that devastated the livestock of that continent, my security team and I were constantly confronted by a process intended to prevent the virus from spreading around the world through travellers like us. In one airport, where we were well known and were handled differently because of security, the woman in charge of protocol led us toward the gate to the aircraft. Stepping through the door, she soaked her shoes in the footbath that killed the virus. My first bodyguard did the same before she said to me, "General, you'll get your shoes all wet if you do that, step over here." In one action, a well-meaning person, not understanding the long-term consequences of her actions, rendered a multimillion-dollar process ineffective. My team accused me for months after of being the sole distributor (no pun intended) of the foot-and-mouth disease virus worldwide.

A funnier and slightly risqué story again illustrates how a process can be undermined unless the hearts and minds of the people are onside. A very successful restaurant, considered the place to be seen, put great value on having the most hygienic environment in which meals were prepared, served and enjoyed. The process was so visible that it became much discussed by the patrons. One man even mentioned this to the waiter. "This place is incredibly clean," he said.

"Yes," said the waiter, "we are all about cleanliness. Everything must sparkle, and we have guidelines to ensure that it stays that way. The staff must be clean, we all wear gloves to handle everything and, even with gloves on, we still must use the silver tongs we each carry to handle any food. In fact, we are so clean," he continued in a conspiratorial whisper, "that when I go to the latrine, I'm not permitted to handle myself. I must use the string hanging in my pants, with a loop in it . . . you get the picture."

Everyone at the table oohed and aahed except one man at the table, who said, "How do you get it back in your pants?"

"I don't know about the rest of the guys," said the waiter, "but I use the silver tongs."

The best-planned and most meticulously thought-out process in the world can be defeated by the lowest person on the organizational totem pole, unless he or she understands the reasoning behind that process and agrees with it.

For every one of those managers who focus on process, there is another (if not two others) who spends her time worrying about her rank vis-à-vis her fellow workers. Such managers are often obsessed by their position within the hierarchy and the perks that go with it: the corner office, the number of committees and boards they sit on, social events that require their presence, personal staff that demand their constant supervision and car and valet service that seek to satisfy their every whim. Those people, often unconsciously, consider that only they exist in the team, forgetting what we were all taught in school sports: that there is no "I" in "team."

Process, if utilized in a positive manner, can help get things done. I constantly think about turning negative situations into positive ones. If you overprocess, you send a very real message to people that their every action in the course of doing their jobs will be guided, controlled and watched. The message is that any act of imagination or initiative is pointless, possibly even dangerous. Try going to a beach in Ontario, a prime example of overprocessing. It's not about what you can do; it's about what you can't: don't litter, don't drink, don't be there after dark, don't play music. Spinning the situation more positively (as in, please respect cleaner beaches and keep them that way) might seem like a small change, but I have always believed a positive spin helps people take responsibility for their actions and apply themselves to making things work. Besides, there's something about constraint that makes the devil in me simply want to do exactly the opposite of what I'm being told.

Process is the call to worship of the weak, the short-sighted, the careerist and the bully in any group—usually people trying to ensure their personal survival. Process is linked closely to risk aversion and is most often used by managers who fear their own shadows as a way of ensuring they never have to make a decision or put their careers or reputations on the line. It almost always, insidiously, fails to bring about results. Committee structure, sign-off sheets, levels of authority, program names, a "table" to which one can bring issues and designs with the complexity of computer flow charts—these are the altars for worship during ten-hour workdays.

CHAPTER 7

TECHNOLOGY IS ALWAYS EXPENSIVE BUT IS NOT ALWAYS THE ANSWER

A common failing of leaders who misunderstand or underestimate the importance of focusing on their people is to focus on technology, which often goes hand in hand with a focus on process. Those who rely on technology seek the advantages of speed and connectivity to ensure productivity. But technology is not cheap and, without the network of the right people with the right aspirations and strategic focus, it can amount to hundreds of millions of dollars wasted. It can consume organizations of people with bringing into service the next generation or upgrade and can actually diminish an organization's ability to produce. After all, if the latest, most expensive technology merely brings you to the next roadblock that much faster, allowing more questions to be asked and more inane options to be considered, when good people know they are irrelevant, what has it achieved? It has eaten up the money critical for training, education, infrastructure and pay raises, among other things, without delivering added value.

We never got this right in the Canadian Forces. We spent hundreds of millions of dollars in developmental systems—standalone, secure, and every other system, all unlinked to each other—and failed to fundamentally change the way we conducted operations. Far from enabling commanders at sea, in the air or on the ground to be more responsive, agile, lethal and effective, most of the money spent allowed a greater management of detail by managers in Ottawa, usually detail that should be the prerogative of tactical commanders. The result was, at the very least, zero gain that cost untold sums. The comparison of communications over several hundred years is telling.

In July 1798, when high-tech meant the sail as a means of propulsion, Admiral Horatio Nelson was preparing to engage the French fleet at the mouth of the Nile River, at the eastern end of the Mediterranean Sea. Usually independent in the extreme and operating within a strategic vision, Nelson felt he needed one decision from their Lordships at the Admiralty in London, his bosses. He penned his request on a single sheet of paper and handed it to his best frigate captain, who then set sail across the Mediterranean, through the Strait of Gibraltar, up the Bay of Biscay and into the River Thames to the docks, where a fast rider seized the missive and delivered it, minutes later, to their Lordships. They considered the request, made a decision, penned their reply on the back of the original request and gave the piece of paper back to the fast rider. Back to the docks it went, to the ship's captain, down the Thames, across the bay, through the straits, and . . . six weeks after having penned his request, Nelson had his response handed to him.

Compare that to now, in Afghanistan, where Canada's commander, Brigadier-General Dean Milner, sits in a command post that is the equal of those in any science-fiction film. With real-time feed from UAVs (unmanned aerial vehicles), satellites, aircraft and troops on the ground, juxtaposed with human intelligence reports that provide environmental assessments on things such as weather and clear knowledge, at a glance, of where friend and foe are, Milner has only to lean forward in his seat and speak to enter a request to Ottawa into his computer system, verify that the voice recognition program says what he wants it to say and hit the send button.

Instantly, with that touch of the button, the request is transmitted via satellites to the same system in Ottawa where the staff officers, using similar computers, consider the request, give a heads-up to the commanders involved, analyze the requirement, develop options, bring these options forward for consideration and decision (always saving work by staying in that same computer system), brief their bosses, capture the discussion and resultant decision, verify that the prepared response to Milner is the decision actually meant to be delivered and, with a push of a button, in a nanosecond send the decision on Milner's request to Kandahar—six weeks later! The point is clear. Despite the hundreds of millions of dollars spent on technological upgrades—and the intervening hundreds of years—the commander on the ground, operating within a mission statement, guidelines, commanders' guidance, the rule of law and a government's vision, had not been enabled. Ottawa's aversion to risk and its ability to peer into tactical detail that truly was meaningless in Ottawa led to a lot of time being spent there, rather than at the sharp end. Ottawa and its mandarins thought they could run the mission in Afghanistan, or any other mission, from a distance, by peering through the equivalent of a ten-thousand-kilometre straw and tinkering with a ten-thousand-kilometre screwdriver.

This was starkly illustrated for me not long after becoming Chief of the Defence Staff. Early one morning my phone at home rang. It was the Operations Centre duty officer, relaying a request from the Canadian commander in Afghanistan, who was asking permission for four Canadian specialists to leave Kabul and move to the next province to do crater analysis for the Americans. An IED (improvised explosive device) had detonated in the American area of operations and the Americans wanted as much information from the remnants of the bomb as possible. They did not have people with the necessary skill sets immediately available, and for once the Canadians did. Travelling by helicopter with US security into a secured area, for only a few hours' work—I was puzzled as to why I was being asked permission for this. It seemed a no-brainer to me. In addition to helping our NATO allies, we would learn more about the deadly IEDs; the threat was minimal and the commander in theatre had recommended it. "Understood, sir," said the young major on the phone, "but these are the rules in place. Any movement of CF personnel outside our own area of ops must be approved by you." I told him to go ahead and went back to sleep.

It was after that phone call that I decided we were going to change how we handled these missions. In my view, our commanders around the world had their missions, my guidance and the appropriate authority and were accountable in various ways for their actions. They had the resources and the option of asking for more resources, and they knew far more about the reasons, benefits and tactical situation of a mission such as sending four specialists out into an American area than I or anyone else in Ottawa did.

"It's their job," I said to my team. "That's why we prepare them generally over twenty years and specifically over this last year. We have faith in them and can assess their performance routinely. If they cannot make decisions like this, we'll find people to be commanders who can."

What had happened, of course, was that the commanders were champing at the bit to do exactly that, to make those decisions and take responsibility for them, but they had been prohibited by Ottawa. We started changing this culture immediately.

I was taught as a young officer and leader to use a maximum of one-third of one's time for analysis, reconnaissance, planning and preparation and to ensure that your subordinates have at least two-thirds of the time available to be able to do their jobs. Better technology, leading to quicker gathering, collation and assessment of facts, should make that figure even more weighted to those who act rather than to those who plan. That is, senior leaders should probably spend less than one-quarter of the time available, giving most of it to those who do the deeds for us.

The technology beast rears its head every single day, and many companies and organizations appear incapable of containing it. Frustration, the waste of incredible amounts of money and a dysfunctional group often result. When I read recently that the new focus of the Public Service of Canada renewal would be technology, I shuddered. Not having achieved a vision, a strategy worthy of the agency's name, much less the right people enabled in the right human network, that focus (technology) will distract from the very real challenges and waste billions of dollars.

CHAPTER 8

THE 95/5 RULE

I made a point of being among the people I led as much as possible, which allowed me to get to know them and give them my attention. As brigade commander in Petawawa, Ontario, with some four thousand soldiers under my command, I spent at least half of each day at work among the soldiers in the units that made up my command. The returns and rewards of being visible and knowing what was going on were phenomenal. Walking about is an underestimated principle of leadership, and it can directly contribute to keeping your focus where it belongs: on your people. Spend at least half of each day with those who do what you ask them to. Spending time with the people who followed me allowed me to focus on the great people who were making our units successful. But occasionally, I, like all other leaders, became focused on the "problem children"—those people who were dragging the organization down—and it often took me a long while to realize what was happening.

When I was commanding a squadron of tanks in Germany in the early 1980s, I was focused on the job. One day I went to the small orderly room where the squadron clerk was dealing with the routine administrative paperwork of several soldiers. I found what I wanted and then, as I was leaving, spoke to a young soldier who had been waiting patiently.

"Corporal Park," I said, "how's it going?"

"Good, sir," he responded, "except for this nagging pay issue that refuses to be resolved. I'm sure you know all about it, though."

I did not know about it, and I was embarrassed to admit it. This problem was incredibly important to this young soldier, but I had been dragged into the fine details of military law, spending about 95 percent of my time on the small handful of soldiers under my command who had been charged with impaired driving, had failed the physical fitness test or been getting into one difficulty after another. Corporal Park, an excellent tank driver and soldier, had given me a wake-up call. He had confidence in me, but I was letting him down by not spending my time on those, like him, who were quietly doing their jobs and carrying the squadron and me so well.

I was not spending my time looking after the 115 soldiers in my squadron who worked hard each and every day, won each fight and made us all proud to be soldiers and Canadians. Instead, I was spending most of my waking hours worrying about those very few who weighed us down. My day was eaten up by administrative procedures to deal with those few ill-disciplined soldiers: a couple with alcohol abuse problems, another who consistently failed his physical fitness test and a fourth who combined the problems of the others. Out of 120 Canadian men, these four were the ones weighing the squadron down and creating a perception in the eyes of external observers that was extremely negative. That perception had serious negative implications for all of us.

I was determined to reverse the trend by spending the majority of my time looking after those who made us all look good. Those who give you so much of their bodies and minds deserve nothing less from you in return. Those who become lamprey eels, sucking from the body of your organization, need to be cut away, cast off and forgotten. Give those who have had difficulties help to recover and repair themselves, but don't get sucked into wasting your time on them at the expense of others if they themselves are not serious participants in the recovery effort. Sometimes ruthlessness is a prerequisite for a leader; otherwise you cannot be fair to all.

From that point on I tried to use the 95/5 percent rule, spending 95 percent of my time on the people who made the organization successful overall, those who made me proud to come to work each day and who usually asked for nothing in return other than respect. I tried—and I admit not always successfully—to spend not more than 5 percent of my time on those who were a burden.

The 95/5 rule applies to any organization: Spend 95 percent of your time looking after those who make your organization successful and 5 percent or less of your time on those who drag you down. Of course, season this rule with a healthy dose of compassion for those who are a part of the backbone of the company but need temporary support. When someone who has given you much, carried you and the organization for either lengthy or difficult periods, needs a little help, that is when you get a chance to do right by them. If you seize that opportunity, it inspires everyone else in your team because it tells them that when they need you, you will be there for them as they have been there for you.

To me, the most important thing I could do as a leader was to give back to the men and women who gave their all for me. I saw more examples than I can relate of those who did not do this, and each one of these examples underlined what a negative impact it can have on an organization—and made giving back to my people even more important to me as a leader. I will never forget, early in my career in the army, one soldier, who was much older and more experienced than most of his comrades, an excellent man, whose wife developed cancer. He began missing a lot of days at work. One of his immediate superiors, a captain, called the soldier into his office and went on at length and with much ruthless enthusiasm about how if he could not focus on his job he would be released from the Canadian Forces. I listened to the captain's cold assessment of a job that he said had to be done, indeed would not have been done without this captain, and did not believe any of it. The soldier had given his all, and now, in the most frightening days of his and his wife's lives, needed us—and we were not there for him. The Forces actually added to his stress by threatening him and abandoning him and his family. The captain even bragged about his tough approach.

To make matters worse, the soldier's performance differed completely from that of the captain, who got himself returned home early from every training exercise or deployment the regiment went on. There was invariably an illness, involving either him or someone in his family, a family emergency of some kind or something else that called him away from his duty during training events. Being the cynical subalterns that we were, we made bets when deploying on when the captain would go home. He was denying the very support that he expected from his superiors to those for whom he had responsibility. This was unacceptable and, in my view, unethical leadership from the captain and the bosses who let him get away with this behaviour. The message is, look after those who have helped build your organization; by doing so you can inspire those who are building the future.

You as a leader must focus on people: those who work for you and with you, and those for whom you work. Develop solid relationships with them. Work constantly to set them up for success and enable them to succeed. Focus them on long-term and intermediate objectives. Do all those things necessary to motivate and inspire them and get their bodies and minds working for your objectives. Give them credit for their work, protect them from blame in failure, enable them to apply their talents, sustain them during tough times and recognize and reward their successes.

You cannot do any of what I suggest unless you know those who follow you, and that means you have to spend time with them. And not with the energy-draining anchors who turn up in any group, those who destroy your passion with their pessimism, see dark clouds at every turn, sap your and your team's energy and turn what could be world-class teams into perennial cellar dwellers. Don't wait for such people to destroy your organization. Identify them and, if you can, get rid of them as quickly as possible. Spend your time on the majority of your people, who are working hard and helping your team achieve success. Remember, it's all about people, and you cannot go far wrong if that is where you spend the bulk of your energy.

71

CHAPTER 9

WHEN RISK MANAGEMENT BECOMES RISK AVERSION

Risk management comes in many forms, but the long-term intent is generally the same: to minimize anything that can prevent you and your team from achieving your vision or that detracts from you having the intended effect and producing tangible results, in both the long and short term.

In military organizations, the term "risk management" is seldom if ever used, but the intent is the same. Unfortunately, over these last two decades we in the Canadian Forces found ourselves falling into the trap of turning our risk-management processes—no matter what we called them—into risk aversion. That is to say, everything we did became about control, rather than getting the result we wanted, achieving our mission or doing what either we knew had to be done or what we had been told we had to do.

The control process came in many guises: personnel, financial, infrastructure, rules of engagement (rules that define when, under what circumstances and with what weapons our soldiers overseas can warn or kill people), reporting procedures, movement policies and much more. These became the focus of most of our effort, and so much time was spent on them that we often forgot the overall vision and the strategic effect we were after. When the bosses focus on something—in this case, all those processes—everybody else tends to also focus on it and, as a result, control became the mission rather than the goal. Let me give you an example.

In the Balkans in the 1990s, the Canadian Forces had a mission to help implement the Dayton Peace Accords in the bloody chaos of the former Yugoslavia, specifically in Bosnia, with some spillover into Croatia, since much of the support for our deployed troops, and the troops themselves, had to come through that country. A Canadian commander (usually a colonel) was theoretically in charge of the mission. Obviously, some money had to be spent to train, move, house and feed our soldiers doing the actual job, which included building base camps, consisting of modular tents augmented by existing local buildings, which were usually in poor repair after several years of civil war. One of our contingents of soldiers repaired one such building by putting in a floor that, according to Ottawa, was a little too luxurious. This may have been true despite the fact that the repair of the building and installation of the floor had offered a significant amount of work to the local men and women and made all of them friends and protectors of Canadians.

The response to our spending a small amount of money was predictable. Instead of viewing the flooring purchase as a good thing in the bigger picture for the Canadian Forces' efforts in Bosnia, the staff in Ottawa essentially removed all spending authority from the in-theatre commander. Among the other national commanders who were part of the same NATO division (which I commanded in 2000–2001), our commander was powerless to do what we all agreed was necessary. The British commander could spend up to a half million pounds without having to consult with London. The Dutch commander had a similar budget. But when the commanders identified high-value needs, the Canadian response was always, "I'll have to ask Ottawa."

In short, the risk or control process had now morphed into a risk-aversion equation, which undermined completely what we were trying to achieve at the strategic and tactical levels in Bosnia on behalf of Canada. While already spending billions, we worried so much about spending a few more dollars that we ended up wasting that money by losing the potential gains. Our commander was undermined and his credibility destroyed— and with it, the credibility of Canada's efforts. It was the ultimate control by a six-thousand-kilometre screwdriver from Ottawa, and it was detrimental to Canada's credibility and influence internationally.

We were all, in those days, focused on control, rather than enabling. I was educated one day by a personal hero of mine, Lieutenant-General Ray Crabbe, on how you can do both at the same time and still keep your eye on your long-term goal. During a tactical exercise in Petawawa, Ontario, commanders from each of the brigade units and their leadership teams (the lieutenant-colonels who commanded them through to the young lieutenants who ran the platoons) used a big map to plan and work through a military operation. The question we were discussing was control: specifically, what control measures were to be used. I was leading the discussion and took the group of about a hundred or more through every possible scenario. How, for example, we kept units from advancing too quickly and making themselves vulnerable, from wandering into another unit's territory and potentially causing "blue on blue" (friendly fire) engagements, from getting bogged down in useless fights and so on. As I ran through the enormous list of things that we did not permit our commanders to do, it soon became clear, even to me, that we worried about risks rather than focusing on getting the mission done.

Ray stood up and took over the discussion. With his good humour, he quickly put it all together. "Your mission," he said, "is to take the objective—the high, dominating ground on our side of the river—and then be prepared to cross that river to attack further." The best way to achieve this, he explained, is to walk through with your commanders what you want to achieve so that they understand it completely and can act independently when things go to hell in a hand basket, why it is important to achieve it, and then how you want to do it. Start at the beginning, go through the advance step by step after clearly stating what your target is, talk about the possible situations that can occur and ensure your team is in your mind. Only by doing that can you give them the confidence that allows them to apply their talents completely and to respond to the unexpected. ("Remember," Ray would say, "no plan ever survives contact with the enemy.") This is greater risk management than anything else you can do. If they understand the what and the why and have a good feel from you, their leader, as to the how, then you have set conditions for success and, at the same time, minimized the risk to its lowest possible level.

The response of the commanders back in Ottawa to the monies that had perhaps been unwisely spent in Bosnia should have been to review the vision and objectives, and confirm that the commander on the ground understood them. He should have had a good review of the what, why and how and been told to smarten up, get on with his mission and use the brain God had given him. And if that didn't work, he should have been fired and someone else brought in to do the job, someone who understood the intent and how to work within it. Instead, the control process to eliminate risk intensified to the point that the ultimate risk was realized—we lost credibility and essentially failed in what we were trying to achieve.

At the strategic level, the NATO mission in Afghanistan is an excellent example of where risk management, designed to minimize distraction and detraction from achieving a vision or mission, can run amok and, through risk aversion, set conditions for failure.

The United States, assisted by several allies but not officially by NATO, had struck the Taliban in Afghanistan within weeks of the 9/11 attacks on the World Trade Center, after receiving confirmation that the assault had been planned by al Qaeda from Afghanistan, where Osama bin Laden and his terrorists were being sheltered by Mullah Omar and the Taliban. Over the next several years, following a process laid out in Bonn, Germany, in December 2001, an Afghan interim government led by interim president Hamid Karzai was installed and Western nations piled on to support the establishment of a peaceful and stable Afghanistan. The secretary general of NATO, George Robertson, had watched the helplessness of the alliance—its wandering in the wilderness now that its raison d'être, the Warsaw Pact and Soviet Union, had disappeared—and saw the future: NATO would have to find a mission to prove its value or disappear. "Out of area (meaning outside the western European basin) or out of business" became the cry of the day.

Yet, despite government leaders supporting NATO's taking on increasing responsibility in Afghanistan and eventually the military mission for the entire country, they neither wanted the risks that came with being able to do that job nor were willing to provide the resources, particularly the troops, to do it. They wanted the credibility and the kudos that came from doing the mission without actually having to do it. Thus was born the strategy to expand the NATO mission from the first nexus, the capital Kabul, across the north of the country and eventually through the south until the NATO area and Afghanistan were the same, by using provincial reconstruction teams (PRTs). A PRT would avoid the risks of military operations, battle casualties and enormously expensive and sizable deployments and instead offer advice and a few bucks for some reconstruction. Hence, the vision would be achieved with very little risk, and that risk would be ruthlessly managed.

The irony, of course, of the world's largest and possibly only military alliance electing to demonstrate its relevance in the post-9/11 world by launching a reconstruction mission seemed to be lost on most people. The risk was low, at least as assessed in the capitals of Europe, and the payback was potentially enormous. Get on with it, said NATO Headquarters in Brussels.

Unfortunately, every set of rules I ever applied to dangerous operations included this one: The enemy has a vote. The overwhelming need in Afghanistan was for security and the forces to provide it. Thus, for six years, NATO, always under pressure and always late to the game, screamed for more and more troops from the same nations that had supported its flawed risk-management strategy from the start. The result was that the alliance lurched from near-disaster to near-disaster. Strategic leadership was reduced to begging for a few more helicopters, troops, trainers or police as ways to avoid complete failure, which was what the strategy had now become. Its vision, confirming the alliance's relevance to its members, was being sought without accepting any risk and ended up creating the highest risk possible: complete failure.

Dr. Barnett Rubin, an American who knows Afghanistan about as well as anybody, said once that this need to have a risk-free approach meant that, once in, "NATO was condemned to success in Afghanistan." That is to say, the alliance could not leave without having been successful because it would mean the end of its existence. NATO's constant loss of credibility during the past six years does not fill one with confidence that success will be its eventual prize. Risk management turned risk aversion has created the greatest risk of all.

At the tactical or local level, risk-management processes become the most common weapons of bullying, indecisive or insecure managers who call themselves leaders and are a burden on those who are so unfortunate as to work for them. Under such bosses, and there are many (I said once that I had learned probably two-thirds of anything I ever knew about leadership from bad examples), the guiding principle is: Don't stick your head above the parapet, because someone will shoot at you. This principle leads to a survivalist mentality, a determination to not do anything or not have anything done that might draw attention to you, at least nothing that might fail during his or her time in a certain appointment or office. In Ottawa, a failure could be career-ending. Wait it out, avoid risk, look and sound good, butter up those above you in appointment and rank and, at all costs, survive. Subordinates, particularly those many eager, talented and imaginative men and women whom I met so often, figuratively die from frustration on the doorstep of risk-adverse managers, those who seek only to survive until their next promotion removes them from the danger of being associated with anything that might fail.

My point is simple. Risk management is a commonsense tool really meant to make sure nothing deters you from achieving your vision. The best risk management is taking people into your mind: what it is you are trying to achieve, why you need to achieve it and what you perceive the best way to do this is. Then, with basic principles and guidance (what we in the military called "commander's guidance"), those you lead will feel confident that they can bring all their energy and talents to bear. Yes, when dealing with things like money and technology, specific regulations are needed, but if you have not brought the people you lead onside to the greater aim and logic, no regulation will reduce the chance of them doing things that create difficulties or failure. Ensure in all you do, including risk management, that you use your common sense and that your actions are not actually increasing your risk by preventing anything at all from getting done.

CHAPTER 10

PERPETUAL OPTIMISM IS A FORCE MULTIPLIER

If you present an image to those in your charge that the weight of the world is on your shoulders, that you have perhaps lost confidence in your mission, that you are broken in spirit if not in body and that you are pessimistic about the immediate or long-term future, those men and women will project the same image. How can you expect them to be optimistic, energized by confidence and a belief in the future, if you yourself are not? Your job, your responsibility as a leader, is to be optimistic and to communicate that optimism to those who follow you as part of enabling them to be successful. Indeed, you might ask yourself why you are a leader if you don't behave like one.

People work better, think better and relate to others better when they are happy and buoyant than they do when they are sad, troubled, insecure or cynical. What you do as a leader can have an enormous effect on that. Just think about it: if you walk down the street and smile at ten people walking toward you, nine will likely smile back. After all, it takes the same energy to smile as it does to frown. I do believe we can change people's approach to life, even if just for a few seconds, with the power of only a smile. I tested this hypothesis constantly on operations, particularly in Afghanistan, among a people whose adult faces mask their emotions almost completely. I would look at someone from the vehicle or while on foot until I caught his eye and then I would smile. And it was incredible: during all my time in Afghanistan—all those times I smiled—I was never disappointed by not getting a positive response.

I sometimes think that in Canada we need to be reminded just how good a life we live, how fortunate we are to live in such a great country and such an affluent society. Because all too often in Canada we look at the silver lining in the cloud that cover our skies and search until we find its small, dark lining and then focus on that dark lining to the exclusion of all else. In fact, many of us tend to focus on it until we become cantankerous and pessimistic.

Yet, we have more reason to be perpetually optimistic than anybody else in the world. I say this a lot to Canadians because, again, I believe they need to be reminded of it and adjust their attitudes. We live in a country with rights and privileges that are only a fantasy for about 80 percent of the world's population. And those rights and privileges, extensive and complete, are enshrined in our Charter of Rights to ensure that no man, woman or child, regardless of colour, ethnicity or sex, is ever left behind. We live in a country where the rule of law, the fundamental framework guiding the interactions of peoples who live together, exists, when it does not in more than 50 percent, or perhaps a lot more, of the world. After having visited, lived in and worked in close to seventy countries, believe me, I can attest that this is special. What is even more special about Canada—and almost certainly we are one of a handful of societies like this—is that we see the rule of law as only the minimum standard for human behaviour. We actually expect a lot more from adults. Few countries can boast of that characteristic.

This was a subject at a reception my wife, Joyce, and I recently attended. I remarked that, in our very ordinary neighbourhood in Ottawa, after more than nine years of living there, we have seen a police car on our street only about six times. Getting slightly pompous about this good record of law and order, I was taken down a notch by my wife, who piped up, "And you were responsible for about three of those appearances."

Of course, even in Canada we occasionally fail to measure up to the rule of law, but when we do, we have the most professional police, legal and judicial systems in the world to help us get back on track. Beat on the Royal Canadian Mounted Police all you want, criticize lenient judges and tell jokes about lawyers, but after having seen the offerings throughout the rest of the world, I know of what I speak. When I see one of those professional young Canadians wearing the uniform of the RCMP stopping traffic on a highway, listen to an Ottawa Police Services constable deal with homeless youth and see lawyers argue in front of the Supreme Court of Canada, I am content that we have the most professional of the professionals in the world working on our behalf and I am proud. Yes, things don't always go right, but we implicitly trust those symbols of the rule of law in our country because they have earned that trust. We can continually improve, but the trust is there.

Think of the other things that put us at the top of the world (often ranked there by the United Nations annually). They include phenomenal cradle-to-grave medical care, despite the beating it takes for political partisan purposes south of the Canada-US border; social networks to help catch those falling and set them back to a road of recovery; and, funding all of that, an economy based on successful entrepreneurship and leadership that is as stable as any in the world, richer than most and resting on a banking system that emerged as the world's number-one system during the 2008–09 worldwide financial implosion. I constantly say to men and women in TD Bank Financial Group and other banks that, after the solid performance of our banks in the last two years, if they cannot market themselves as part of the solid base of the best nation in the world, they are missing the opportunity of a lifetime. Of course, listening to politicians and journalists rail against the banks, you could understand their reluctance to push their advantage. But that just makes it all the funnier to see Canada's politicians now, after beating on those banks constantly for years, defend them against other countries seeking to punish their own banks that failed them. Ours did not fail us.

Nowhere else in the world is affluence spread so evenly throughout the population. Our middle class makes up most of the nation's 35 million inhabitants. To help us stay this way, we have the best education system in the world. So, in our great country, why would you not start each day with a smile on your face, a song on your lips and an optimism about that day and every one to come that is infectious to everyone you encounter?

And that's based just on what we are and have in our country, without considering what we are not or don't have. Again, I have said to tens of thousands of Canadians that we don't have to worry because we do not live in a country such as Afghanistan, where more than 15 percent of women giving birth die and close to 25 percent of newborns die at birth. These birth mother and birth mortality rates are among the highest in the world and devastate families there. In Canada, rare is the person who knows the mortality rates in his or her city or province, and that's a good thing. The rates are so low that we simply expect every mother to survive giving birth and every healthy child who is born to live. Anything but that actually catches our attention.

We also don't have to worry about our children stepping on or triggering IEDs (improvised explosive devices), including anti-personnel mines. In Afghanistan, children missing one or more feet or legs are common. There are so many of these children that merchants selling second-hand shoes can make a living selling footwear for one foot or the other if they do not have a matching pair. Thirty years of unrelenting extremism and violence have seen to that.

Canadians also don't have to worry about whether our children can go to school or will be prevented from doing so simply because no school exists or because violent men such as those in the Taliban stop them because the students are female. We certainly do not have to worry about public beatings or executions in our society, whereas in Afghanistan men were beaten if their beards were not long enough to be grasped in the fist and still show hair beneath it, women were whipped if their hands showed from underneath their burkas and they had fingernail polish on, and women were beaten if their shoes made a clicking sound on the stones in the street when they walked. Worse than all of this, women were executed during half time at a soccer game in front of thousands of people simply because they had been seen in the presence of men who were not from their immediate families. If you need more reminding of just how optimistic we should perpetually be, if you're a man, think about it when you look in the mirror as you shave each day, and if you are a woman, whenever your heels click on the pavement. We live the best lives in the world, in the best country in the world, and should be on top of the world each and every day.

Perpetual optimism costs nothing, is worth millions and has the power to transform people almost instantly. Most people are this way because they are optimists, and many of us have experienced the startling change that comes over an organization when an optimist assumes a leadership role from someone who is not. At a cost of nothing, she is empowering with energy, confidence and passion everyone around her, and empowering them as a group to achieve an effect out of all proportion to the numbers. What a return on investment.

It's natural, sadly, to sometimes forget why you should be perpetually optimistic and what a difference it can make. My face can set into lines, if I'm not careful, that can seem a little frightening to some, so I try to prevent that. Sometimes, though, things happen that make it difficult if not impossible to maintain my optimism. That occurred all too many times during my military career, but none was so disturbing as when we lost multiple soldiers during attacks in Afghanistan and in training events back here in Canada. Twice we lost six soldiers in attacks, once on Easter Sunday 2007, while I and most of the leadership of Canada were at Vimy Ridge participating in commemoration and remembrance ceremonies to honour the brave Canadians who fought there ninety years earlier, and again on 4 July 2007, while I was at home in Ottawa. Equally daunting was the fatal training event on 13 July 2006 off the east coast of Canada, when during a night exercise of the search and rescue team one of the Cormorant helicopters crashed into the ocean, killing three of the SAR Techs on board.

At Vimy, we got word late of the attack on Sunday morning, 8 April, while preparing for lunch and events in Amiens that afternoon, where Canadian soldiers were to be given the freedom of the city. Andy Leslie, the army commander, called me aside to say that the National Defence Headquarters command centre had been trying to reach me or my aide on the phone (unfortunately, we were in a dead zone) to report that we had lost six soldiers in the previous hours. The shock was enormous. My thoughts as always went first to those we had lost, their battle buddies who would be in shock and disbelief, and their families, whose lives had been changed forever. Second thoughts concerned how we needed to maintain the priorities of looking after those involved—lost soldiers, battle buddies and the families back in Canada—to the exclusion of other interests. In the close confines of Vimy, with media, civilians, military, bureaucrats and politicians galore, word of this loss would get out quickly. But, as I soon found out, we were having difficulty locating the families, scattered throughout Canada, to break the sad news. We certainly did not want that news to reach them through the media or in any other public manner.

I pushed to maintain my cheerfulness, but while others oohed over the beautiful weather and exquisite architecture of Amiens and aahed over the military parade to receive the honour, I was dragged down into what felt like the depths of despair. Not helping was significant pressure from senior bureaucrats accompanying the Canadian prime minister, who wanted him to announce the loss at his speech that evening. Without any understanding of the devastating effects of an IED, the resulting chaos at night (which it was in Afghanistan) and the need to be certain that we had correctly identified how many were dead, who they were, who was wounded and what families remained to be notified, they just wanted to get on with the announcement. Regardless of the fact that, if unable to confirm that the families had been notified of the losses, such an announcement meant twenty-five hundred families in Canada would go into crisis. Making the announcement, according to the Privy Council officer, was more important than those other things. It was almost impossible for me, as the leader of the Canadian Forces, to maintain any kind of optimism, no matter how much I tried. The lack of concern for people—the first priority being a politician's image—disgusted me.

The second time I really focused on perpetual optimism and its importance was just a few months later, on 4 July. At about 3 a.m., at home and sleeping, I received a phone call informing me that we had again lost six soldiers in an attack. Joyce, beside me, had also been awakened by the ringing of the phone. We both were unable to get back to sleep, so I finally got up and headed into National Defence Headquarters. It was a Wednesday morning and the day of our weekly senior leadership team meeting.

We convened at 8 a.m., and the director of staff, Bruce Donaldson, briefed worldwide operations to the group of twenty or so senior military commanders and public servants.

The first item briefed was the attack and, with the assistance of photos and a timeline, Bruce detailed what had occurred (or at least as best we knew), displayed pictures of the soldiers who had been killed and described the consequent actions and state of affairs. As he spoke I glanced around the table. It was clear that everyone was dramatically affected: faces were long, expressions strained, bodies tense or slumped, and several people had tears running down their faces. As a group we looked beaten. It was my job to ensure that we didn't get perceived that way once we had left that room.

After Bruce had finished his brief, I took over. "Look," I said, "we've got a lot of responsibility as leaders, and here is how we are going to meet it. First, we're going to look after those soldiers who died and ensure that their bodies are recovered, returned to their loved ones, treated with dignity and given all the honour that they have earned. Second, we will look after their battle buddies, who are wounded, physically and mentally, and ensure that they have all the leadership, care and support they need. Third, we will look after the families who have endured these terrible losses. We will wrap our arms, figuratively and literally, around them and support them through what are going to be the worst days of their lives. There is no qualifier on that support, in terms of amount, type or time. And, from the perspective of the group at this table, we are going to do all of that in the next thirty seconds or so. If we don't and leave this room looking the way we now do, beaten, with loss of faith and confidence in what we are doing, in two hours every person in the National Capital Region who works for us will look that way, and in twenty-four hours the entire CF and their families will too. We will have failed to provide them the leadership that they need now and that is our responsibility to provide. We must give them the confidence that, despite our terrible losses, our mission is just and our commitment unwavering. We will have failed those who look to us for that, and that we cannot do."

Leaving the room immediately afterward without looking like I had been crushed, had lost confidence or was beaten was difficult, but throughout the next hours as I moved around National Defence Headquarters and Ottawa, I put a spring into my step, kept my face from descending into a grimace (I won't say I had a smile because that would not be true) and said hello to everybody I met. Everyone else did likewise because they were conscientious and professional leaders who understood just how essential this was and how important their roles were. We got through that day, and the next, and continued to provide the optimistic leadership our men and women expected from us. That was our job.

Hopefully, the days when your optimism is tested will not be frequent and you will not be tested as brutally. Learning from us, you will be able to pass your test with flying colours. Remember, the people around you go as you do, and if you are perceived as broken, they will respond that way also. We have uncountable reasons to be optimistic, so make sure that you are, every day.

CHAPTER 11

PASSION PAYS

Passion, to me, is your character in action, in a visible and demonstrative manner that shows your perpetual optimism. Passion, of course, relies heavily on emotion, and it is emotion that separates us from animals and robots. If you are not passionate about what you do, how you do it and the people with whom you do it, you are not applying your character and hence have left the emotive side of you are at home. There is significant evidence that passion contributes to healthy lives, less stress and happier workplaces that accomplish more, and more efficiently.

Enthusiasm is the most evident form of passion you can use to fire others up to do their job and apply their own characters to the job. About the only career advice I gave my two sons as they considered what they might do in life was to do something they loved. "Life's too short," I said, "to do something that you don't like or even hate. I see people every day who hate their work, can't wait to get away from work and don't want to go back to it. Even though they don't live as long as those who love what they do, I'm sure that for them, life is so unhappy that it seems twice as long." I still believe that and simply recommend that if you cannot be passionate about what you do every day, your lack of passion will define you and you will not succeed. Be passionate, bring your character to the job, bring your emotions to do things that you love, fire up others the same way as you yourself are and combine this with the perpetual optimism about life, our country and the company's prospects, to help build a winning environment and team that make you even more passionate. You can see where this might go. A friend of mine, who loved being a soldier, used to say every day as he went about soldiering, "If this doesn't light your fire, your wood's all wet." Make sure your wood is dry, and that your fire is lit.

PART 2

LEADERS THINK LONG

GET STARTED

When you are a leader, those in your charge want certain things from you as much as or more than you want things from them. First, they want a reason to follow you beyond just getting a regular paycheque or simply because it's their job or, even worse, because that's just the way it is. That approach simply won't work. That will get you either their bodies or their minds, but not both.

For years as a young general officer in the Canadian Forces, I attended the Chief of the Defence Staff's annual general and flag officer seminars. We would spend two days or so on issues of substance, including where we were going in the military (for example, how we were going to build the Canadian Forces on our extremely limited budgets or, more often than not, what we were going to cut), and also on issues that were largely irrelevant (for example, NATO, which in its present form and approach had become almost completely meaningless to us). This was a welcome relief from the tough, real-world questions we had to face. I went to each of these events with one simple question in mind for the Chief of the Defence Staff: Why should I follow you for another year?

The men and women who work for you and who look to you for leadership will be asking you exactly that question, whether they say it out loud or not. They will want to know why they should follow you. They will want to be convinced of your logic, and one of the ways to have them understand that logic and to convince them to continue to follow you is to express that you think long, that you have a vision for where you and your people are going and what you want to achieve.

And if you do think long, is that vision sufficiently captivating to bring people with you? Or are you just another person standing at the head of the table, droning on far too long, expecting people to follow you and to work to support you because you have a nameplate on your office door and the power to promote, hire or fire them? Convince your team that they should follow you because of the value you bring to them as people. You must convince them that you're a leader, that you know where "we" should go and that following you is exactly what they want to do.

Getting started as a leader is key; it's critical that your actions are visible as soon as you take charge. I'm talking about days, not weeks, after you assume your role—the sooner the better. If you have not started making fundamental changes within your first three to four months on the job, you're not ever going to do it. By the end of the first trimester, if you haven't started making changes, if not actual progress on implementing those changes, a lack of inertia will set in. Items on your agenda won't seem so urgent, and the problems won't seem to be urgent either. You'll begin having extreme difficulty seeing how you could possibly do anything without upsetting the apple cart. When that happens, you yourself have become part of the problem. Upset the apple cart early and publicly.

When I was appointed to the top job in the Canadian Forces, we were determined to learn from all that we had gone through and to do better. That is, we were not condemning our predecessors or destroying what they had done (you don't know how things were for people until you have walked a mile in their shoes) but using their work as our base to project ourselves forward. In fact, I believe that the major accomplishment of those leaders was that the Canadian Forces survived. Given all that had been imposed on us in the 1990s and what had gone before, it is almost miraculous that our military did not collapse upon itself. Thanks to our predecessors, we survived and could begin implementing the changes we all wanted to make.

We started with the leader—me. I articulated my vision to the senior leadership team of the Forces, in Cornwall, Ontario, where I had gathered the team to lay out the way ahead for us. I did not use a single PowerPoint slide, but instead simply spoke of the changing world, the rearward focus that had really hurt our chances of being considered relevant by most Canadians, what I viewed as our goals and the logic that had led me to these conclusions. As I spoke I drew, with the image projected onto a whiteboard screen. Drawing allowed me to work my line of logic and seemed, at least to me, to be very effective at helping others follow my presentation. PowerPoint slides wouldn't have worked quite so well.

The detailed preparation for this presentation had taken place in the previous weeks, before I was officially announced as the new Chief of the Defence Staff, in the basement of my house with trusted confidantes from the navy, army and air force. After the announcement was made, our work continued at National Defence Headquarters, working with the deputy minister, Ward Elcock, and with Vince Rigby, from the policy group in the Department of National Defence, and his team. My good friend and Vice Chief of the Defence Staff Ron Buck joined in on the discussion. Thus, upon assuming command, I was as ready as I could be to act quickly.

Within two weeks of taking command, we had called together that group of senior leaders—not only the generals and the admirals but also, under the authority of Deputy Minister Elcock, the senior civilian leaders in the department, making sure to include more than just senior officers. We also invited the most senior non-commissioned officers, that is, the senior soldiers, sailors and airmen and airwomen from each of the army, navy and air force and the major commands, who brought with them experience, smarts, common sense and a no-bull attitude. We came together to discuss the vision I had articulated in a three-day session at the Transport Training Centre of Canada, in Cornwall, Ontario.

I stood up to speak the first morning, laying out where I thought we had been and were, and my concerns about catastrophic failure. I then moved on to what I believed we needed to do, and why. It took me the first morning to go through it all. General discussion, complete with criticism, advice and belly-aching, followed. We broke into small groups or syndicates, each assigned specific questions to discuss. Finally, we returned to a full session, presented the responses (some of them brutally honest) and had a "come to Jesus" discussion (in which the light shines brightly and the problems, with solutions, are clear) about my now reframed vision. We came away from the seminar with our vision for the Canadian Forces and the future. The senior leaders had, by and large, bought in, and what we were trying to achieve had become ours, not just mine. I vividly remember senior lead- ers, including Lieutenant-General Rick Findley, the deputy com- mander of NORAD in Colorado, and Lieutenant-General Mike Maisonneuve, Chief of Staff for NATO's Allied Command Trans- formation in Virginia, standing up and saying that they had been beating around this bush before and had failed to fundamentally change the Canadian Forces. Those leaders, and others, were now saying that this would now be our vision, that it was about time we had one and that it was ours to be successful with or fail at. They were keen to implement the vision within the guidelines I gave. We left that seminar with "our" vision for the Canadian Forces, the first time in my life in uniform that I had seen this kind of unified approach.

We had worked hard to make sure the vision reflected prag- matically, with common sense and in a way that drew us all in, what the Canadian Forces was trying to achieve for Canada. After a lot of work, some false starts and much advice from our public affairs folks, we articulated a vision that was short and to the point. It was strategic, guiding but not limiting, and some- thing our men and women in uniform and, indeed, all Canadi- ans could understand and identify with. I simply said that from then on, "We are after the Vimy effect." More than ninety years after that battle, and the valour Canadian soldiers displayed on the battlefield, the Battle of Vimy Ridge continues to shape and inspire Canadians across the nation. The inspiration comes from how the fight was won, not necessarily what it achieved. And so, how Vimy was won became the guiding light of our vision.

The battle was won, first, because Canadians fought under a unified command where the pride of our nation was at stake: if the attack faltered, Canada's young reputation would be shattered. If Canadians brought together under a single commander failed to succeed in their mission, it would be their failure, not that of other Allies, and blame would not be shared. As I once told our prime minister, Paul Martin, wanting to share the podium during times of success or victory means you also have to be prepared to share it during defeat or disaster.

But while the risk to our fledgling nation was high, so was the opportunity. Fighting and winning as Canadians would give us the profile and visibility that, as just one more cog in the massive military offensives in Europe, we lacked but desperately wanted. That profile, if we were successful, would give us credibility, and that credibility would give a nation of just 11 million people a seat at the table when the postwar decisions on Europe were made. It would strategically position Canada to influence the postwar world in the way that we wanted, but until then, could not get. For the first time since 1st Canadian Division headed to England in September 1914, and then on to continental Europe in later fall 1914, all four Canadian divisions were fighting under one flag, one commander and with one objective.

It had been Canada's goal throughout the war to do this, but Vimy was the first time it was able to happen. After the First World

War, we did not experience that unified Canadian approach again until late in the Second World War, when First Canadian Army fought up through the Allied flanks in northwest Europe, through Belgium and the Netherlands, under unbelievably terrible conditions, while being much ignored by the rest of the world. In the numerous operations since then, Canadians rarely fought as one entity, under one commander. With that decreased visibility, we did not have the credibility and say in shaping the affairs of the world commensurate with our sacrifice. In Vimy we did, and the consequent signature by Canada on the Treaty of Versailles to end the First World War was a direct result.

In the years immediately after 2005, we wanted Canadians operating internationally to replicate what occurred at Vimy—all Canadians operating under one commander, representing our country, whether by air, land or sea, so that our operations and sacrifices would be visible and credible, and give us the stature to shape world events. This was a distinct change from what we had managed to accomplish in the previous decade of worldwide operations, and we needed to link it to something tangible for our nation to understand it.

The leaders of the Canadian Forces believed that was exactly what Canada needed in 2005. For years, but particularly in the 1990s, we had frittered away Canadian impact through "contributions" to larger missions. We put whole battle groups into the Balkans—thousands of soldiers, along with naval and air forces—but we did it in such a way as to be practically invisible. One battle group of fourteen hundred troops was in Bosnia, near Sarajevo, under one command structure. Another was in Croatia under a second UN command headquarters. Our logistics battalion was on the coast of Croatia under national command. A naval flotilla, consisting at times of a submarine, destroyer, frigate and supply ship with embarked aircraft, sailed the Adriatic to enforce the UN weapons embargo and were under a fourth command structure. Air assets in Aviano, Italy, flew constant missions into Sarajevo and elsewhere under a fifth command structure.

Those command structures and the way we did our business meant that our enormous and costly contribution—measured not just in dollars but, far more important, in the lives of our men and women—was essentially invisible and gave us little profile, very little credibility and certainly no seat at the table to help set the course for Eastern Europe, straining to break free from forty plus years of Communist domination. Our national interests and values were not considered and definitely not furthered.

We believed this had to change—and would change with our new vision. Canada had to ruthlessly position military forces, as part of a larger Team Canada, to represent our interests, epitomize our values and give us the opportunity to shape the world in a way we believed was right for us and all of humanity. Thus, the Canadian Forces' international deployments had to be carefully considered, aimed at achieving maximum effect for Canada, under a single Canadian command, and not just contributions divided up among the command structures of other nations, the UN or NATO. We had to do all that—on behalf of our country, its people and international stability—in such a way that, ninety years later, Canadians would remember how we had done our job and would be so proud of it that we too would have become a guiding light for them.

But unified command, or working together, was about more than having Canadians fighting under their own flag.

It was about what 1st Canadian Corps did in the First World War in having all combat and supporting arms, artillery, infantry, engineers, communicators and so on work as one team. We wanted to take that a step further and emphasize that Canada's small armed forces had to work as one team of air, land, sea and special forces if we wanted it to make the strategic impact that a G8 nation deserved and needed in order to continue being a G8 nation. Thus, our battle cry was to make our people proud to be in the Canadian Forces but not so proud as to be incapable of working together as Canadians under one command. Canada had to ensure that one visible, capable force represented it on every mission despite pressures to do otherwise (no different from the pressures at Vimy and, for that matter, during the entirety of the Second World War).

Visible leadership for the Canadian Forces was critical. For too long we had meandered aimlessly, perceived as essentially just another department of government. The perception among the rank and file was that, outside of their immediate leaders—the officers who were right there beside them in the field or on the bases—they were being managed, not led. Outside of their unit, most soldiers couldn't name their commanders and leaders and, consequently, had little faith in their decisions. As conditions continued to deteriorate throughout the 1980s and 1990s, the rank and file felt no relationship with those strategic leaders and the little faith became no faith. There were notable exceptions, but lack of confidence ran very high.

Second, the leadership of the Canadian Corps during the preparations and attack at Vimy was visible, involved and committed. Although this had been a tendency in most Canadian units during the first year of the First World War, it was not the case elsewhere; tales abound of generals relaxing in country châteaux while their men died in icy, muddy, rat- and flea-infested trenches. But, in fact, some Canadian leaders, like division commanders Currie, Turner and Mercer, spent a large amount of time at the front. Indeed, just several months before the assault, Mercer was killed in the forward trenches by an artillery burst. During the lead-up and the attack, that leadership was even more present, with the commanders instilling confidence by their quiet determination and competence, understanding the environment where their men lived and modifying the attack even at the last moment to take advantage of small changes in the ground that they themselves had seen. From Sir Julian Byng, the Corps commander, to the division and all the subordinate commanders, they set the example, leading and exhorting their men from the front.

We wanted our men and women—in the air, on the land and at sea—to know their leaders and to be able to see and approach them during the most stressful times in a very similar manner. Equally important, we wanted our leaders to understand, through being there themselves, the conditions under which our men and women had to work. You can talk about equipment shortcomings or maintenance difficulties until the cows come home, but visiting one unit and seeing most of its fifty fighting vehicles parked against the fence because there is not enough money or spare parts makes an entirely different impact.

Thus, we felt that our vision needed to include a distinct move away from a staff-centric Canadian Forces, where commanders were surrounded and almost overwhelmed by their administrators and staff officers to the point where they virtually disappeared. That led to a situation where most initiatives had to come up through a ponderous and painful staff process that took months or even years to complete. I used to joke that if I issued an order when I first took command, I had no idea where it would go, who would ever get it and what it would actually say when it finally arrived. That needed to be changed, and we felt that we needed a leadership and command-centric culture, where visible leaders occupied command positions and were publicly given the authority, responsibility and accountability to carry out specific missions. I expected those leaders not only to be visible to those they led, to communicate and work with all of them, but also to be visible to all Canadians. After all, the lives of our men and women rested on the decisions of those commanders.

At Vimy there was a respect and care for people that had not been obvious in many other military forces up to that point in the war. Soldiers were often seen as expendable and indeed the attitude among many senior officers of the First World War was, "It takes 14,000 casualties to train a division commander"—a frightening belief that in order for a commander to learn what he needed to win, he would have to lose most of his division and have it replaced. It was appalling!

In the Canadian Corps, the soldiers were valued, and steps were taken to ensure their success and, at the same time, reduce the risks to them as they launched the attack. Routes were thoroughly laid out—a significant complex of tunnels was covertly dug in the chalky ground leading up Vimy Ridge to allow soldiers to approach the jump-off points under cover, with protection from artillery fire to the very last second. Hospitals were established in the small rooms dug off the main tunnels so that care could be provided as quickly as possible to the wounded. So many things were done to improve protection, reduce casualties and provide confidence to those attacking that each soldier was quietly bolstered in his confidence that he could make the attack for Canada and survive. That had not been the case during other offensives on the Western Front. By the end of the Battle of the Somme, with almost a million Allied casualties, that care had far-reaching impacts. The respect for soldiers as valued, mature men was novel and something we wanted to emphasize in the modern Canadian Forces, where many of our past practices looked and smelled like bureaucratic and managerial approaches, not leadership. The perfect sign of that, in my view, was our adoption of the terrible term "human resources" to describe those men and women of flesh and blood, with dreams, aspirations, insecurities and all the other human characteristics. That term is a direct insult to anyone who considers himself or herself a mature, responsible adult, reducing people to numbers.

Perhaps more important than any of the other important points that made Vimy our vision was that the Canadian Corps became a learning organization. That had not really factored into military thinking until then and was immediately brought to a revolutionary level by our predecessors. The German tactics in previous assaults, experienced by the British and French at Vimy and elsewhere, were studied and analyzed. The Canadian gunners picked apart the way the Germans used their artillery and came up with a list of their predictable tendencies, leading to an effective campaign that destroyed or neutralized much of their killing artillery even before the battle began. Canadian and Allied tactics in previous battles were dissected, their successes and failures noted. The Canadian commanders learned important lessons, and incorporated them into the training that would make their new tactics successful. Large-scale models of the ridge, overlaid by known German defensive positions (from information gained through foot patrols, air reconnaissance and balloon observers) were built, and each and every soldier, leader and team practised their roles time and time again until all knew what to do no matter the situation.

Becoming a learning organization was tough but essential, and emulating the Vimy example was one way to lever our progress in that direction. Over the previous decade we had the chance to learn many lessons on operations in the chaotic post–Cold War world, but very few of them had stayed with us. We had observed lessons from places like Bosnia, Somalia and Rwanda but by and large had not really made the changes necessary to ensure they were part of our culture; we had not learned from them, we had merely observed them. The lessons that had been captured tended to be of the minor—and in hindsight fairly obvious—kind, such as, don't take an alcoholic on an overseas operation, since if that person has a drinking problem in Canada, he or she will continue to have a drinking problem when deployed, which made for a potential disaster when we were involved in sensitive and sometimes violent situations.

To change this, we sought at the tactical and strategic levels to turn these lessons into doctrinal changes. We altered our training, which helped us to win, hands down, every fight we got into after that, not with hockey scores of 3–2, but 100–0 if possible. Vimy had taught us the power of learning those lessons.

The leaders and soldiers in the spring of 1917 brought their combined experience to bear in fighting the Germans, devised new tactics that took their strengths, the ground and German tactics into consideration and then—a first for the First World War—rehearsed those tactics in detail. Every soldier in the 1st Canadian Corps, regardless of rank, understood the message, his role and the reason for the kind of approach that was to be taken. We wanted our Vimy heritage to shape current and future operations in the same way.

I believed this was important to us in the present-day Canadian Forces because I also believed that we did *not* learn. We discussed many things but we did not truly use these points from past operations or training to change our policy or training. We had not been, *as the Canadian Forces*, in the Balkans conducting operations for fifteen years; we had simply been there for thirty separate six-month rotations, each almost uniquely prepared based on present doctrine. Early efforts to change that had seen mostly local success, but the strategic challenges had made it impossible to get anywhere near where we had to be. Becoming a learning organization was key to success and a fundamental base for increasing credibility internationally and therefore critical to attaining greater influence for Canada around the world.

We achieved many things in the last years and none more important than visibly becoming a learning organization. In Afghanistan, the technical analysis team would be onsite within two hours of an attack or operation. Within four hours, its initial findings would be shared with the deployed troops so that they understood that something new had occurred, and why. Within four days, the team's more detailed report would reach the army collective training centre in Wainwright, Alberta, where the next soldiers to deploy were preparing, and it would shape their training. This approach shaped every part of the Canadian Forces. In fact, we believed that the troops in each deploying rotation were better prepared for the operation than those whom they were replacing, despite their six to eight months of hands-on experience.

Lastly, we wanted the Vimy heritage to reassert itself in helping us empower all those in uniform so that we could get the full value of their training, education, imagination, observations and personal will. We wanted their bodies and minds, something that had happened only rarely during the years of benign training and hapless missions. Starting by empowering commanders with as much authority and responsibility as they could bear, to conduct operations either at home or abroad, we wanted that same attitude of empowerment to be extended to all of those incredible national treasures that serve our country in our nation's uniform.

When asked by young soldiers and non-commissioned officers in Afghanistan, sailors on ships in the Persian Gulf and aircrew in cockpits around the world how I was going to ensure the continuation of what we had started in the Canadian Forces after my departure as Chief of the Defence Staff, my answer was always that I was not. It was their responsibility as soldiers, sailors and aircrew, as leaders, officers and commanders, to continue what they believed in. We could accomplish that only if those young men and women were asked to achieve their goals—rather than being just told what to do—and then given the tools to achieve them.

Thus, our vision ("We are after the Vimy effect") summed up in six words a rich background, history, significance and understanding by all who heard it. This vision did not represent pages of bureaucratese, doublespeak and political correctness. It was a rallying cry to the greatness that our nation had once experienced and could again. It defined in human terms what we in the Canadian Forces were seeking to accomplish and it resonated with everyone in uniform.

TACTICS WITHOUT STRATEGY BRINGS FAILURE

Everyone wants to be focused on long-term goals, to be part of a larger vision. That's how they get through each day: believing that it all will add up to something fundamentally important. Without that long-term thought, it's difficult to get anything done. Sometimes, it's simply impossible.

Short-term activities must be guided by that long-term view and at the very least a broad strategic approach if they are to be effective. That is, the major routes to achieve your vision must be thought through, articulated and then used to guide daily, or tactical, activities. Without this, the result is often mass confusion, inefficiency and failure. At minimum, you need a long-term approach to make coherent short-term decisions and, equally important, you need a long-term approach to avoid making incoherent short-term decisions.

In the Canadian Forces, we had difficulty thinking in those long-term, strategic ways. It was not from lack of understanding, smarts or desire, but simply because of pressure. We had been thoroughly chewed up by devastated budgets, aging equipment, scandals and contempt from Canadians who took no ownership of us, combined with more operations being conducted on the backs of fewer people in uniform. We certainly were not "Canada's" armed forces in the view of most Canadians. The terrible toll of that perfect storm almost broke us. We were always on the run, usually at sprint speed, and trying to prevent failure each day rather than guarantee success. Far from criticizing leaders of that day, I commend them, because without their guidance we would have broken down entirely. Our mere survival in those terrible times is a compliment to each of them. But it was impossible in a country that simply wanted contributions from us, especially cost savings, and that had no vision for an armed force, to be able to define our raison d'être ourselves. Now we could.

But sadly, we paid an enormous price for failing to think long. The logic in all we did was not apparent and therefore could be attacked. Risk avoidance became a focal point. We responded to everyday activities, often with knee-jerk reactions, rather than shaping them with the guidance of where we were trying to go. For example, we bought new aircraft without the people or spare parts to fly and maintain them. We cancelled purchases of other spare parts for old aircraft, yet kept them in service much longer than expected and then were frustrated because those spare parts, as was the case with the C-130 Hercules tactical transport aircraft, had a three-year wait time. It meant that those aircraft were available less and less, while the cost to run them—we paid through the nose for parts wherever we could find them—went up and up. Incoherency comes from failing to guide daily operations with a strategic thought process, and we lived it.

Soldiers, sailors, airmen and airwomen, and their families, not enamoured of what was happening, simply looked for a future outside the forces. Our best people started to leave. For those who stayed, cynicism, frustration and low morale were the order of the day and led inevitably to an even shorter-term focus that severely exacerbated the problem.

Equally troubling, those Canadians outside the Forces abounded who wanted to shape the military forces of our country for their own, sometimes nefarious, interests. Without a strategic thought process and the solid logic that goes with that to defeat them, their interference whittled away at everything from military justice to how we educate young leaders. Not thinking long, not shaping everything we did with a strategic view and, more precisely, thinking short and thinking tactically, was brutally damaging to the Canadian Forces.

Changing the image of the Canadian Forces and connecting to Canadians became part of our thinking long. Fifteen years from now (the short term, in our vision), when young boys and girls who are just today starting junior kindergarten are ready to start down career paths, they have to at least consider Canada's military as one of those paths. If they do not, with the enormous shift in our demographics that sees an aging population and decreasing numbers of young people to fill the increasing numbers of jobs in the market, we will have failed. It will be too late to change and improve the image in the year those kids start to graduate; it had to be set in place right then. We had to synchronize the linking of our vision to our nation's past with our Recruit the Nation strategy.

As a follower, I demanded a vision from my leaders. Few were able to provide a vision that allowed me to follow them wholeheartedly. I didn't want the kind of approach we see in bureaucracies, corporations or institutions that state what to avoid. I didn't want to read page after page of mission statements that most people stopped reading after the first sentence. Political correctness run amok can lead to useless managerial exercises that consume time, energy and resources and in the end fail to produce anything with lasting impact. The only saving grace in a government department in Ottawa was that most visions were paper exercises that were ignored completely in the capital.

After we had defined our vision, the logic behind it and then the general approach to start achieving it, we laid out the strategic thought process. Under the umbrella of achieving that effect, we said we would build the command systems, based on those commanders who would allow us to do our job well, starting here in Canada, so that we worked as one Canadian Forces, not as separate entities. Second, we would build a task force from air, land and sea forces that would visibly demonstrate how we would do things in the future and be ready to deploy immediately if our government needed it. Third, we started building the task forces that would replace those who were the first to deploy and continue a mission over the longer period. Fourth, we were changing our approach to the Special Forces, growing and reshaping them in various ways to help reach that vision. Fifth, we were going to have more people, who would be better prepared and better equipped (even though many of the details of how that would be accomplished remained to be defined). Those strategic routes enabled our everyday work to proceed coherently.

Our vision was brief, not a seventeen-page document that would not have been read beyond the first few lines. It really did drive, in every way imaginable, how we in the Canadian Forces went about our business. Your vision for your team should do the same. Really, it's part of your job and probably the most difficult aspect of it. When you are up to your ass in alligators, have already received a painful bite or two and are anticipating more painful bites, as a leader you can't allow yourself to be distracted. It is your responsibility to remember that your job is to drain the swamp.

CHAPTER 14

MAKE COHERENT SHORT-TERM DECISIONS

You cannot make coherent short-term decisions unless you know what you are trying to achieve in the longer term and make each decision in that context. You need to be guided by your vision. Unfortunately, we in the military have many examples of how we didn't do this and all too few positive examples. Whether it was how we "contributed" to operations in the past, getting little benefit for a huge cost; how we handled our downsizing in the 1990s, when we cut recruiting, paying young kids whom we had just trained to leave the Canadian Forces; or how we failed to prioritize our equipment needs and let the most valuable pieces be sold off because the Government of Canada had no idea as to what it wanted its armed forces to be, except cheaper, our bad short-term decisions are legendary.

The perfect example of an incoherent short-term decision, made under huge pressures without any guiding principles from a long-term view, is the fate of our Chinook helicopters. The Chinooks, big double-rotor transport helicopters, are real workhorses. Able to carry enormous loads, sling equipment beneath them, fly long missions, operate day or night, lift in "hot and high" environments and keep flying even with significant combat damage, they were as valuable in Canada for help to Canadians across the North or during natural disasters like the 1999 eastern Ontario and Quebec ice storm as they were in international hotspots like Afghanistan.

We had eight of them flying for Canada when the budget cuts hit the Canadian Forces in 1994. The air force, intent on protecting its fleet of jet fighters, felt that because the Chinooks carried army gear, and the air force's budget had been cut by 38 percent, it couldn't afford them. If the army wanted Chinooks, it could pay for them. The army, trying to protect its infantry battalions, said that its budget had been cut by 39 percent, and if the air force wanted the Chinooks, *it* could pay for them.

Without a guiding vision to shape the subsequent decisions, nobody fought for the capability that the Chinooks represented, a capability that was worth its considerable weight in gold. So we sold our eight operational Chinooks to the Royal Dutch Air Force. Years later, nothing pissed me off more than arriving in Afghanistan, on Kandahar Airfield, and having a Dutch Chinook pick up me and my team to fly us out to visit our troops deployed in the forward areas. In would come the helicopter, with the Dutch Air Force roundel on the fuselage, but you could still see the outline of the Canadian flag underneath it. Each one of those former Canadian helicopters was a tangible reminder that you cannot make coherent short-term decisions without thinking long and knowing what you want to achieve.

I observed another good example of short-term thinking in 1988, when the Edmonton Oilers traded Wayne Gretzky, the team's franchise player and probably the greatest hockey player of his day, to the Los Angeles Kings. The trade made sense in the short run for Oilers' owner Peter Pocklington, who got the $15 million his floundering business empire needed badly, for a player who was at the peak of his great play-making powers but who wasn't getting any younger or more valuable. The Oilers got some good players in return and actually managed to win the Stanley Cup without the Great One two seasons after the Gretzky trade, but it was never the same overpowering team that it had been under the leadership of number 99.

As a lifelong Toronto Maple Leafs fan, I was pleased, of course, to see the dominant team of the 1980s lose its star player (although I would have been even more pleased to see Wayne in a Toronto jersey). But for Edmonton fans, that trade was a disaster. The dynasty that had ruled the NHL for so many years came crashing down, and within a couple of years the rest of the team that had been built up around Gretzky—great players like Mark Messier, Jari Kurri and Esa Tikkanen—left for greener pastures. The Oilers, and to an extent all small-market Canadian teams, have never quite recovered. The decision to trade Gretzky was a good move for Pocklington in the short term, but because he wasn't thinking long it ended up destroying the franchise that had made him rich and famous. Attendance at Oilers games dwindled, and eventually Pocklington went bankrupt and was forced to sell the team. The short-term gain was based on incoherent thinking and disappeared almost immediately.

There are numerous other reasons for thinking long, difficult though it is to do (as politicians tell me frequently). On the personnel side—providing my commanders with the motivated and trained young Canadians they need to do their jobs—the challenge was enormous. In Canada, where the demographic of our population is, as I mentioned earlier, shifting to reflect the large percentage of "mature" or (like me) old people, every institution, corporation, company and organization is in a war for talent. We all want the best of our society's shrinking number of young men and women. We knew that unless we built the credibility of the Canadian Forces needed to get those people, we would fail. Without people we would be able to do nothing, and if we wanted to ensure that we'd get them and still have them with us in twenty years, we had to get to work.

This led to our Recruit the Nation strategy. We wanted every Canadian to feel that the Canadian Armed Forces was *their* Canadian Armed Forces. We wanted Canada's moms and dads to publicly claim their sons and daughters who served in uniform. In fact, I used to say to my command team, "If we cannot market Canada's sons and daughters back to Canada's moms and dads, we ought to move over and let someone who can do what must be the easiest job in the world come in and do it." In the Recruit the Nation strategy, we weren't after new recruits for our ranks, or new money, political decisions or any of the other short-term, superficial support that we needed. We wanted that too, of course, but mostly we wanted ownership by Canadians, knowing that where our population focused, the politicians would sooner or later follow.

"Get involved!" I've said publicly to Canadians many times. "If you like us, support us, and if you don't, get involved and help change us. You do not have the privilege of ignoring your armed forces and then throwing rocks at us when something goes wrong."

The renaissance in Canada of the Canadian Forces—Canadians viewing the country's armed forces positively—is in large part because of the Recruit the Nation strategy. It was the result of a lot of people working hard to achieve short-term goals, raising the Canadian Forces' profile with the public in hundreds of little and not-so-little ways. But thinking anything but long would not have accomplished the strategy.

GET BODIES AND MINDS

I have never forgotten how challenging it can be to convince people to fully commit to a common goal. I learned quickly that the drudgery of daily tasks could elicit only so much excitement. People really get fired up if they know that a task is going to amount to something more. In short, they want a vision, and they want to know their roles in getting to that vision so that they can use all their innate qualities to make it happen. They want to be challenged and inspired to live their lives fully, to contribute to something essentially good and to feel they are a part of it—sometimes even playing a leadership role. They want to live every day with purpose, moving toward that faraway time in the rocking chair on the back porch when they will remember a life well lived. They don't want to do a task just because they're told to or because they are paid to. They may do the task, usually to the minimum standard, but doing the tasks they believe are necessary to achieve something great in the longer term is dramatically different.

Harold Ballard's ownership of the Toronto Maple Leafs—the Leafs' "decade of darkness"—provides many examples of how not to lead. Ballard's erratic and autocratic tenure at the helm of what had been a great NHL team (and still is, in my view) is a particularly good case study of how you can own your employees' bodies but not their minds. He once called his team captain, Darryl Sittler, "the son I never had," but his treatment of his players soon soured that relationship. Ballard took the attitude that he was paying plenty to Sittler, one of the most talented forwards in NHL history, and Sittler should be happy just to have a job. When Sittler, not surprisingly, disagreed and agitated for better pay and contracts for players, Ballard took every opportunity to belittle and humiliate him, including trading Sittler's good friend Lanny McDonald (another NHL legend). Ballard's actions and his reputation sent the Leafs into a downward spiral that took them decades to recover from. Ballard may have owned the players' contracts—their bodies—but his treatment of them made certain that he didn't own their minds, and didn't inspire them to play at the level of which they were capable. They wouldn't give him "110 percent," to use the sports cliché that separates winning teams from perpetual also-rans. Many NHL players refused even to consider moving to the Leafs because of Ballard, and the team did not manage a winning record until after Ballard's death in 1990.

I shudder these days when hearing of union-company agreements that detail, to the second it sometimes seems, how much time things must take, when changes must occur and the precision with which human interaction should take place. It is abnormal and leads invariably to the body doing a fine job, while that ever so valuable mind is on vacation. Thinking long helps change all of that—to your benefit as leader, to the benefit of your company or organization and, perhaps most important, to the benefit of those who work for and follow you.

CHAPTER 16

NEVER WASTE A CRISIS

"Get to the other side of the valley," says Ed Clark, president and CEO of TD Bank Financial Group, and I echo that statement, though emphasize it in a slightly different way. If you are a leader and have followed, in your own individual fashion, any of the tips in this book so far, you have a vision and have laid out a route, with the major interchanges detailed at least, to achieve it. You, and those who follow, are proceeding ever onward and upward toward that vision.

Murphy's Law is alive and well, however. Disaster can strike and crisis may ensue. This is when you should excel. The builders of the *Titanic* said, "She's unsinkable," only to have the power of Mother Nature, in the form of an iceberg, prove them wrong. When things do go wrong, you have a chance to make things happen more efficiently than ever before. You also have an opportunity to build your credibility as a leader, and this can serve you well in the longer term, because how you behave during a crisis will mark you more in the eyes of followers than almost anything else. Keeping calm, analyzing the events, involving people in the work that needs to be done, thanking those who keep things from exploding out of control, avoiding casting blame and moving steadily toward the practical implementation of concrete steps will solidify your credentials in everyone's eyes. If you do all of the above with common sense, you will be in a position of strength.

A leader's job during crisis is multifaceted and follows very closely the method that emergency medical staff use when dealing with wounded patients: check for breathing, stop the bleeding, keep the casualty from going into shock and get him or her moved along (this is where the similarity ends). Your job as leader is to, yes, deal with the crisis and return to routine business as quickly as possible, but at the same time it is to use everything about that crisis to propel you and your team toward your vision even more quickly than you could move before. You don't want to waste the opportunity crisis offers, and if you have shaped your organization to spend only a little time each day on the routine things, you have the capacity to focus on taking advantage of what is before you.

I think about it this way: a crisis occurs—a financial collapse, a competitor's revolutionary new product hits the market or your company faces adverse legal action—and your company starts getting sidetracked from its strategy. Your first job is to stabilize and prevent freefall. Once you have done that, your second job is to regain a plateau, making positive, visible momentum. Third, use the crisis events to accelerate through the route previously laid out route to achieve your vision even faster. The response to the Red River Flood and to the ice storm in Ontario and Quebec are good examples of where we used a crisis to accomplish more quickly and effectively what we were trying to do. Combat operations in Afghanistan, particularly when we started taking casualties, gave us similar potential. We ensured that the sacrifice made by lost soldiers would have long-lasting and positive effects for the Canadian Forces and Canada, not just for the people of Afghanistan.

When the Red River Flood of 1997 and ice storm of 1998 occurred, the Canadian Forces were still heading downwards in terms of their own morale, the relationship with Canadian society and our pride in wearing Canada's uniform. Canadians had ignored their military for years, noticing us only when we made news in a negative way; the recovery of the Canadian Forces had no momentum. Then suddenly, thousands of outstanding young men and women were out helping Canadians when they needed help the most. That crisis gave us the chance to gain momentum and start building a relationship—and credibility—with the public. Putting those young, fit, energetic, dedicated and imaginative uniformed men and women in front of civilians at every turn, doing the job as opposed to *talking* about doing the job and being absolutely open about what we were trying to do on behalf of those who needed help created momentum first in Winnipeg and then in eastern Ontario and Quebec. That was the beginning. Intuitively we knew we had to move, but for some reason couldn't get started on the journey. It was those crises that jump-started us on that journey.

Even a great tragedy can be an opportunity. In 2003, while our first battle group was deployed in Kabul, Afghanistan, a roadside bomb struck one of our patrols, killing Sergeant Robert Alan

Short and Corporal Robbie Beerenfenger and wounding three others. I was the Chief of the Land Staff at the time, the head of the army, and when I heard the tragic news I immediately determined that we were going to treat our fallen heroes right. And we would take care of their families and their wounded comrades. Most important, we were going to do it all publicly. We held a large and very moving memorial service in Petawawa, where the soldiers were based. Something very similar occurred just over a year prior to that when we had four soldiers killed at Tarnak Farms in Kandahar. When their bodies arrived in Trenton and were then driven to Toronto, along Highway 401, it was the start of an extraordinary outpouring of support from the Canadian public for our soldiers fighting overseas. Although we obviously never planned to benefit from the loss of our soldiers, because we had done things right—dealing with the loss publicly so that all of Canada could grieve along with the families of our fallen heroes—we turned a tragedy into something at least a little positive for the families and the entire Canadian Forces.

You don't want to cause a crisis, because you never know where it will end, but if one does occur and you have prepared your team well, it is one of the better opportunities that a leader gets to make radical change extremely quickly. Go to it.

CHAPTER 17

BUILD ON HISTORY

I can point out places, people and events where our leadership for the Canadian Forces was simply not present, let alone effective; fortunately, I can also point out those places and occasions where we got it right. Building on our history and using what occurred in years past to inspire and sustain us in the present and in the years to come was something that we did get right. Quite frankly, we did it better than any other organization in our country, even those with equally colourful histories. We did it so well, in fact, that Canadian men and women in our nation's uniform were inspired, dedicated and determined to a level that was at times unbelievable. So inspired were they by the men and women who had preceded them in the Canadian Forces or the Canadian Army, the Royal Canadian Navy or the Royal Canadian Air Force, that they would rather lay down their lives than besmirch the valour and glory of these predecessors. When you have dedication and determination like that and can use it in a positive way, you can change the world.

We start early. From the time they appear at a recruiting centre, job applicants are surrounded by the past, present and future. In Canada, unit symbols, inscribed with the battle honours won by their predecessors in the unit through feats of courage and daring that most Canadians know only from TV, go back to the Northwest Rebellion of the mid-1800s. Young soldiers and officers are surrounded by reminders of a glorious past, one that is treated reverently, with tribute paid at every opportunity. Regimental, ship and squadron celebrations and commemorations are held on the anniversaries of momentous events, and all serving men and women, veterans, families and supporters are invited to participate. By the time the first enlistment is up, usually a period of three years, those men and women understand that they have a strong responsibility to carry high the torch that has been handed to them.

When I first arrived at the Royal Canadian Dragoons (RCD), we all had to have a copy of the Regimental History and know the battle honours that had been awarded to formally recognize the major battles in which the Dragoons had fought. Places like South Africa; Amiens in France; Italy; and northwest Europe became known to us as places of valour. For example, for their actions during the regiment's campaign in the Boer War, in South Africa, three members were awarded the Victoria Cross, the highest award for valour in the British Empire. On 7 November 1900, Lieutenant Turner, Lieutenant Cockburn and Sergeant Holland provided an example of devotion to duty by beating off multiple Boer attacks, providing leadership under enemy fire and by rescuing the artillery's guns in the last few seconds before the Boers swarmed over the British position. That resonates with everyone who serves as a Dragoon more than one hundred years later. Every year, in the commemoration and celebration of that valour, the regiment rededicates itself to continue service in that manner. The young officers and troopers understand the importance of their role in carrying on the tradition.

All too often, though, we tend to over time idealize these heroes. But they were anything but perfect. Take my example of Sergeant Ernest "Smokey" Smith, a Canadian who continues to inspire and whom I mentioned in Chapter 2. Smokey joined the Seaforth Highlanders out of Vancouver during the Second World War. He fought in Sicily during the summer of 1943, then up the boot of Italy in 1943 and 1944 and finally finished the war in northwest Europe in 1945. In October 1944, Smokey was a twenty-nine-year-old section commander, with eight soldiers as his responsibility. On 22 October, grabbing two of his soldiers, both wounded, he responded to an attack by several German tanks and self-propelled guns—accompanied by over thirty German soldiers. Using the notoriously unreliable PIAT (projector, infantry, anti-tank) weapon, he knocked out one of the tanks, used his Tommy gun to take out most of the platoon on the ground, crossed the road to find another PIAT, knocked out the second tank and then protected his two soldiers by bringing so much fire to bear that the Germans who could withdrew.

The reason that Smokey is real to me is that, despite his heroics, he wasn't perfect. Immediately after the fight, the commanding officer recommended Smokey for the Victoria Cross and promoted him to corporal, the first rank of a leader. Smokey got terribly drunk to celebrate, got into a fight with a bunch of soldiers from another unit and the next day was demoted to private. Three weeks later, the recommendation for the Victoria Cross went from the Italian theatre of operations to military headquarters in London and the commanding officer decided once again to promote Smokey. In an almost exact rerun of the previous event, Smokey got in trouble and was demoted to private once more. In the next six months, Smokey was promoted to corporal and demoted to private nine times. This guy was a rogue and lived life to the fullest. When he was ordered to Buckingham Palace to receive the Victoria Cross from the hands of the King, the commanding officer, no dummy himself, had Smokey held in the "calaboose" (jail) the night before and then escorted from the front lines of Italy to the front gates of Buckingham Palace by two military policemen just to make sure he did not take a sudden detour to the nearest pub for a beer.

Smokey's example of valour is so powerful because he was so real. Men and women right across the Canadian Forces, and indeed our nation, paid tribute to him in a military funeral when he died in August 2005. He, and countless others like him, have handed the torch to today's generation of soldiers, and those soldiers are visibly intent on holding it high.

Your company or organization is no different. There were heroes who came before you. Their stories can be inspirational to those now part of the company, and it is up to you as a leader to find those examples and share them with the present generation. My experience has been that almost everyone in life wants to understand where they fit in the greater scheme of life beyond themselves. They want to have a history and are ready to carry that history forward. Again, this is a no-cost, no-brainer way of inspiring and encouraging people to bring their bodies and minds, with their values, to the organization to help achieve today's goals.

CHAPTER 18

YOU CAN'T DO IT ALL

One of the most difficult tasks for a leader is to adequately prioritize what he or she wants done and make everyone in the team understand what is important and what can wait. Often, the one or two overwhelmingly key priorities are clear, as are the things that can definitely wait a while. It's those things in between that confound.

Part of the problem in setting clear priorities and identifying what you want done with those things in between is that many people see priorities in black and white. They see them as stand-alone, carrying out priority number one perhaps to the exclusion of all others, when in reality if priorities two, three and four are not also done, priority one was done for naught. I didn't have a "one size fits all" method for defining priorities and enabling people to understand intuitively which work in combination; I just worked at it every day. Consistency is critical, since a focus that changes daily will quickly confuse the organization. Relating those priorities directly to your vision and showing their place in the overall strategy is the most effective way to manage by objective that I know of.

I let myself get shaped by events. When I first assumed the role of Chief of the Defence Staff, my priority was simply to develop a Canadian Forces that could do all that our nation needed and in a way that would make every Canadian proud. Attracting, recruiting and training people were key. Getting the equipment, restoring pride, putting the Forces back into the Canadian psyche and, particularly, changing the way we operated were also all important and difficult priorities. Eventually, too, so was everything that allowed us to operate in this new way. None of these elements could be ignored, and demands from various constituencies for action on one or the other were normal.

Thinking of how to do all this was difficult; actually getting it done was the easy part. What made it easy was having a vision; otherwise we would have had no long-term, strategic focus to guide everything we did, and not just in the doing but also in the way we did it. We knew what needed doing, and that helped to shape our priorities. As Lewis Carroll once said, "If you don't know where you are going, any road will get you there." Well, we knew where we were going and which road to follow, so we could shape all the other events and needs to it, while taking advantage of drive-by opportunities.

As is the case during any change, you need action early. That for me involved getting the senior leaders onside; having money visibly committed to the project; acquiring at least one piece of large, badly needed equipment immediately; and making visible, commonsense organizational change. That, for the most part, was also easy. The money had been committed, in large amounts, based on the prime minister's discussions with me and the minister of defence when I interviewed to become Chief of the Defence Staff several months earlier. I assumed the appointment on 4 February 2005, and in the budget of that same month almost $13 billion had been added for defence. There were many qualifiers—we would get the money over five years and much of it was tied to specific acquisitions—but I was okay with that. We could not have ramped up to spend more money than that any faster, and the list of acquisitions came from us and satisfied our greatest needs. The challenge came in turning that money and commitment into real equipment on the ground, in the air or at sea. Although the frustrations in doing that during the first year were enormous, we more than made up for it in the second year. Our expectations had been met tenfold. After all, we had just come out of the decade of darkness, so simply to have a government that stopped beating us was more than we believed possible. Anything beyond that was powerful.

Finally, we needed to make organizational changes to show we meant business. Now, you already know how I feel about time spent fruitlessly tinkering with organizations, appointments, ranks and other tangible signs of people's positions, but we had some fundamentals completely wrong and had failed to put leaders in clear command appointments, give them missions, support them to execute those missions and then hold them accountable for their missions. Instead, it was difficult to tell the commanders—the leaders—from the staff. The negative impact of this on getting things done was enormous. We could never actually find anyone who was more responsible, authorized and accountable than anybody else. As John F. Kennedy said, "Victory has a thousand fathers, but defeat is an orphan." I wanted to look people in the eye in times of both victory and defeat, and, of course, do my best to help us achieve the former and avoid the latter.

We experienced significant frustration because of multiple people having responsibility for what seemed like the same thing. The US secretary of defense, Donald Rumsfeld, made a comment about the US intelligence community that applied to our situation. Rumsfeld said he wanted "one dog to kick" on intelligence, instead of "a whole kennel." I don't kick dogs or people, but ownership of missions was paramount for me. Thus, we made some early organizational changes, perhaps the most profound since 1968, when the Royal Canadian Navy, the Canadian Army and the Royal Canadian Air Force were unified into one service.

The senior leaders had the opportunity to shape the changes. Some of the work for them came to me from several amazingly astute officers—including Kelly Williams, now a commodore in the navy, and Mike Kampman, now a brigadier-general in the army—who could think objectively, shape those thoughts with practical experience and offer solutions for a murky future. When I gathered the senior leaders in Cornwall, Ontario, within days of taking command, we went through it all: what were the threats of the future, how could we defeat them, what did that mean for us and so on. We left with the vision, a basic strategic roadmap to get us there and, importantly, a commitment to reconvene in just three months' time. In the meantime, we would organize working groups to investigate specific issues; the groups would report at the next meeting with sufficient detail, for each issue we identified, to allow us to make coherent decisions.

The Cornwall discussions led to clear organizational decisions early on, the most important of which was establishing one commander, with appropriate support, who was responsible, authorized and accountable for all international operations; one commander who was similarly empowered for all operations in Canada; one commander for all support operations; and, equally important, one commander for all special forces operations who would work for either of the first two and be supported by the third. Although this organizational structure had been recommended in various forms numerous times, it had never been implemented. This meant, for example, that for the first time in our history we were considering Canada as an operational theatre and setting ourselves up for success in operations to help Canadians directly in a way that we had not done before.

All of the above helped me, and my senior leadership team, peer through the smog of thousands of important factors and actually get started. Soon, though, the need to reconnect to Canadians reared its head so high that we could not ignore it. We were launching our next phase of the mission in Afghanistan by returning to Kandahar province and therefore inserting ourselves into the consciousness of Canadians, whether they were elected political leaders or not. Because with that phase of the mission came casualties.

Dark is the cloud that has no silver lining, and that was so with our combat operations. I had to make some ruthless decisions to get things done, stating in what order the resources, including time and credibility, would be invested, what I would focus on, where the senior leaders needed to focus, and what would be left to others. The loss of young men and women in combat, our wounded and their families made it clear to me where my responsibilities lay.

The mission in Kandahar became my top priority and I will never apologize for that. If we were asking men and women to take on this significantly risky mission, I had to be comfortable setting the conditions for success, and that included lowering the risk to the people involved to the lowest possible level. We had to give them the greatest possible chance to do their job and come home safely.

Second, we clearly needed to change the Canadian Forces as quickly as possible, in order to conduct not only the Afghan mission but others like it in the future. Using the overwhelming need for change in how we did those operations as the front end of a torpedo, we could then drive change to all the other parts of the torpedo. We were not giving Canada the strategic impact it needed, were not achieving the Vimy effect, and we were in a hurry to get those things done.

Third, and equally important, we had to reconnect to Canadians. I viewed that connection as paramount for the long-term health of our country and therefore the Canadian Forces. Canadians did not view us as their armed forces. They felt they really had no stake in us, and most viewed us as a simple waste of dollars that could be used for something important. We had to change that, not to ensure dollars in our budget, not to get new equipment, not to attract recruits, not to get support for military families, but to get all of that and more. That led to us launching the Recruit the Nation strategy. Tying the men and women who serve Canada in our nation's uniform to the rest of the population was key. Connecting the rest of the population to those in uniform was even more critical. This became an enormous piece of work.

Those became my three guiding priorities. I expected many other things to get done, but by and large anything else was the responsibility of subordinate commanders guided by our vision and approach, with my specific guidance as needed. My time, focus, energy and thoughts were on Afghanistan, transforming the Canadian Forces and connecting with Canadians. To the chagrin of many, a person didn't even get into my office if he or she wasn't involved in one of those three priorities. Real life had intruded, and the events involving the lives of men and women who worked for me caused a great crystallization in my thought process. Prioritization became easy.

My point is simple: work hard at the prioritizing, and beware of strategic changes, since continuously lurching left or right from your course can destabilize your team. Be prepared to have your priorities driven by events or take advantage of events to drive them yourself.

PART 3

WHAT WORKS?

THE POWER OF ONE

One person truly can make a difference. Senator Ted Kennedy, when he eulogized his brother Robert, so tragically assassinated in June 1968, said: "My brother need not be idealized, or enlarged in death beyond what he was in life; but be remembered simply as a good and decent man, who saw wrong and tried to right it; saw suffering and tried to heal it; saw war and tried to stop it."

Of course, not everyone is as talented and charismatic as Robert Kennedy, but you, as a leader, can still make just as much of a difference as Kennedy did. Your job is to make things better and to change the world, and to find those people who themselves can change things for the better. Learn to recognize them for the immense effect they can have, and then support and sustain them in their work. They are not always immediately identifiable, and you may really have to work to spot them. But that is simply another reason for getting to know those who work for you.

Those who make a difference are often leaders without a portfolio, that is, people who lead without any formal appointment whatsoever. Two examples influenced me greatly and make the point that any one person, if he or she decides, can change the world. Ideas and ideals when pursued with energy and zest can take hold and change others.

The first example is a woman from Springdale, Newfoundland, a small coastal town in the north-central part of my home province. Her name is Gladys Osmond, and she is a retired Salvation Army officer, age eighty-seven, who lives in the Valley Vista Senior Citizens Home where she maintains an immaculate cottage, crammed with artifacts, messages, trinkets and souvenirs from around the world. Her tiny cottage is a veritable museum of our nation's commitment internationally, full of items sent to her by men and women in the Canadian Forces while they are deployed on missions outside Canada. You see, Gladys writes those serving men and women, the sailors, soldiers, airmen and airwomen, constantly, wherever they are, and they respond. One of the most difficult parts of being away from home on missions in poor and perilous places is remembering that there is a normal life in this great country of ours and that people there have you in their thoughts and prayers. You tend to start thinking, when alone on that dirty, dusty and dangerous trail and someone starts shooting at you, that you are all alone in the world. What Gladys does changes that.

Gladys helps ensure that connection between our country and those we ask to do difficult things for it remains strong. I first received letters from her in 1995 when in Croatia. The newsy letter, talking about the deep snow around her home lingering despite the onset of spring, the first birds chirping and other, minor things that make up our real, normal lives, were accompanied by photographs showing some of what she talked about. Suddenly, eight thousand kilometres from my native island, I was home. Gladys, with her letters, kept me and thousands of others in touch and helped us maintain our centre of gravity while we served in some of the worst conditions imaginable. With her tens of thousands of letters, postage paid for by her, Gladys made a difference.

Her letter writing would have been enough to put Gladys in the hall of heroes, but this woman of action, this leader, did not stop there. In that same retirement home she organized many of the other residents to also write letters. Twenty-five of them, twenty-four women and one man, calling themselves the Granny Brigade, got involved and multiplied the powerful effect that Gladys was having many times over. Joyce and I had the great pleasure to go to Springdale in 2007 and recognize Gladys and the other members of the Granny Brigade for their efforts that have had such impact. I presented the CF Medallion for Distinguished Service to Gladys and the Commander's Commendation to the Granny Brigade for their support. Averaging some 90 years of age, with Bertha at 103 being the oldest, the Granny Brigade was as proud and nervous as teenagers in our presence. Bertha, who was too frail to leave her room, told us when we visited her there that she could no longer see and therefore could no longer write the letters herself, but that she could still tell stories and the others could write and send them on her behalf.

Speaking with each member of the brigade was memorable. One woman commented on the "nice brooch" I was wearing (my medals and ribbons). Each of them was so tickled to be doing something worthwhile, and to be now recognized for it was special indeed. What was also amazing was that Gladys had started using a computer at age eighty-four; now she was on the Internet and connecting to thousands worldwide. I continue to receive emails from her even though I'm retired. Gladys has received an honorary doctorate of letters from Memorial University and has been invested into the Order of Newfoundland, all because she is making a difference. Be a Gladys Osmond, and find the equivalent of the Granny Brigade in your team.

The second person I use as an example of how one person can make a difference is Maureen Eykelenboom, from Comox, British Columbia. I don't know what would be worse: to be on Maureen's side and constantly pushed and prodded to get things done, or not to be on her side and be a target for her efforts. Either way, you quickly realize when you meet her that this is not a woman who suffers fools easily.

I met Maureen on what, I am certain, was the worst day of her life. She was in Trenton, Ontario, waiting to receive the body of her son, Andrew, home from Afghanistan. Andrew, nicknamed Boomer, had been a combat medic on the mission in Kandahar and had written her by email about much of his experience, particularly about the terrible need to help children who had so little. He conducted clinics for kids in every village he went to and was, by himself, making a difference in their lives. "Send me good things for the kids, Mom, because they have nothing," said Andrew in one of his phone calls home. Sadly, after volunteering for a last mission before rotating home, Andrew was killed by a suicide bomber on 11 August 2006.

When I arrived in Trenton, I didn't even get fully through the door before Maureen was in front of me. A diminutive woman physically, her force of personality made her look ten feet tall. With a finger in my chest, she said, "General, we are going to make sure people notice and remember Andrew's sacrifice, aren't we?"

I said, "Yes, Maureen, we are."

Then she said, with her finger almost piercing my chest, "We're going to make sure the good work Andrew believed in continues, aren't we?"

I again replied, "Yes, Maureen, we are."

"General," she said, "you're going to be involved, aren't you?" By now, with the door banging me on my backside and Maureen's finger now heading toward my spine, I knew better than to say anything but "absolutely."

Maureen then seemed to have an adrenaline bleed. She stepped back, relaxed some and said, "General Hillier, did you know that my maiden name was Hillier?"

"Maureen," I said, "I should have guessed. After having been bossed around all my life by Hillier women, starting with my mother, my five sisters, my wife and now continuing with my daughter-in-law, why should you, as a Hillier woman, be any different?"

Maureen, with the support of many, went on to establish Boomer's Legacy and did two major things. First, she raised money to help those in need in Afghanistan, particularly medical help. Second, she organized women to knit wool caps, labelled "Boomer" caps, to keep Afghan children, especially the very young ones, warm. Over these past three years, thousands of hand-knit Boomer caps have been sent overseas, more than 82,590 to date. The Boomer's Legacy effort has also raised $278,000 for the Assistance to Afghanistan Trust Fund, a distribution fund in Kandahar that soldiers can access when they identify an area of need.

Boomer's Legacy has helped purchase much-needed medical supplies and funded life-saving surgeries, bringing unimaginable relief to families who would otherwise continue to suffer. The fund has enabled our soldiers to replace an Afghan farmer's sheep blown up by an IED (improvised explosive device), and given them the means to teach new skills to Afghan people so that they can more effectively support themselves. Through Boomer's Legacy, soldiers have purchased shoes for children in an orphanage who were facing another cold winter barefoot, and much more.

This kind of help—small, focused and precise—tends to directly help about ten people, the members of the immediate family. The effect is incredible, and several hundred thousand people in southern Afghanistan, all of them destitute, have been in some way touched by Maureen and her drive to continue Andrew's work. All this because one woman was determined to continue her son's commitment to making a difference. Be a Maureen in your company, find the Maureens that are out there and help them focus their desires and efforts to make a difference. You, with them, can change the world. Whether that "world" is your company or a team within the company, a town in your home province, another part of the world or, indeed, the world itself, your legacy will be powerful.

RADICAL ASKS DEMAND
RADICAL EVIDENCE

The greatest demonstration of a leader's respect for his or her troops is rational explanation. Walking members of the team through the radical evidence that lead to a radical change demonstrates to those team members that they are fellow citizens, mature and responsible adults worthy of having the logic and the "why" behind the change shared with them. Respect cannot be separated from goodwill, which in this case is expressed by an action, the act of the explanation. You may think that Hillier is losing it here, but none other than Aristotle proffered these thoughts. I believe they are still relevant today.

Change in a company or organization is inevitable, yet it can cause huge problems and untold stress. In the business of soldiering, viewing change, for me, meant looking at the enemy. So, for example, the Taliban we were fighting in Afghanistan would change their tactics, weapons and methods of operation on an almost daily basis as they learned our tactics, studied our defences and sought out our vulnerable spots. They were moving forward. If we were not doing the same—analyzing the environment, assessing the differences and constantly changing our tactics, training procedures and equipment as we learned what worked and what did not—we would fall behind. By maintaining the status quo, when judged against a competitor who is moving forward, you are actually going backward, and that is unacceptable. Change is a fundamental part of everyday life now. There is no going back to more stable, predictable times.

Most of the men and women working for you, however, are likely insecure in times of change or become tired of the process of change itself. The insecurity comes from shifting from the known to the unknown; for example, a change in a process that everyone understands for a new way of doing things, with different steps and requirements. That makes people uncomfortable, and many may feel that their status or place in the company is being undermined or is at risk. Perhaps they are no longer the ones to whom everyone goes for information or who have the insider details of how to get something done, or they no longer control access to the decision makers. Thus, change can be a major stressor for most people; at best, this leads to an unenthusiastic approach to change, at worse, opposition to it. All leaders need to keep this in mind. Even if they had not been made cynical by a rotating group of new managers seizing yet another approach to make their mark in the organization, your people are certainly scared.

Chances are also that they have too often been traumatized by the latest business management techniques or methodology and now view change as the enemy. As someone once said to me, "The only change they want is that which rattles in their pocket." Such an attitude is lethal when you need to change to remain competitive or even survive. It certainly doesn't lend itself to bringing the body, let alone the mind, to work each day. Instead, you get robots, people who are simply waiting until they can move on to less stressful work environments. Given our current demographics where we do not have enough young men and women to meet even the majority of the need, your people can easily find alternatives to you.

For the health of your organization and in order to be successful, you have to bring the doubting Thomases with you. In order to do that, when leading a group through change, you as a leader need to understand the dynamics of the group. My own analysis leads to a general breakdown that I have seen repeated almost everywhere. First, how a group of men and women shape up can be illustrated by a bell curve. In a group of one hundred, there will be three subgroups: the first of about 15 percent at the front leading the change, the second of about 15 percent at the rear resisting the change and, the third, the majority of about 70 percent in the middle, uncommitted—not enthusiastic but not yet resistant. Your challenge is to work with each group and, in particular, to win over the group in the middle.

The first group, those in the front leading change, will be with you on your plans and vision. But that group itself is divided into two approximately equal parts. One half is the power that leads you to succeed. The other half is a drag that can burn out people. That's because the 15 percent at the front end are there for different reasons. The most positive, roughly 8 percent, are there because they have already seen the need and intuitively understand the necessity of change in order to survive, compete and win. They are visionaries themselves. They come from every part of the company and are not necessarily the ones who you would have thought were visionaries. They may be very young or old, loud and boisterous or quiet and introverted. When you talk about radical change to them, they wonder why you didn't see the necessity of such change years ago—what took you, as their leader, so long to get the message and start work. Indeed, they wonder why you have not yet finished the job. This small group is composed of leaders and potential leaders and is extremely valuable.

That group is the lever that will bring the 70 percent of uncommitted onside. Supporting your work, communication and efforts, they can make compelling cases to their peers through demonstration, action or just plain talk, something simply not possible in large groups. As these 8 percent go, so will the 70 percent who are uncertain and waiting to be convinced. Your chances of success increase dramatically if you can enable the 8 percenters to be your ambassadors and the conveyors of the vision. As visionaries, they are your clones, so seize the opportunity and run with it. Lots of time spent with them at the front end of change pays off throughout.

The other half of the 15 percent who lead change, however, can be dangerous to you and your people because they are usually what I call change junkies. They are the people who live for the adrenalin rush of the challenge, throwing overboard staid systems, thriving in the chaos of uncertainty and then moving onto something else in months, weeks, or even just days. Although this can be useful, it is dangerous because any change sets them off, and the line of logic is not necessary to convince them to work. Dangerous change, ungrounded in need and sucking people, energy, time and other resources in already short supply, is as appealing to this group as change based on the most solid evidence and study. They can burn organizations to death quickly, repel talented people and hurtle you and those you lead into an abyss from which recovery and detoxification, usually with intervention, has to be handled by others. So beware the change junkies, fired up by adrenalin over the changes they can be involved in, and the havoc they can cause.

At the other end of the bell curve, the remaining 15 percent who resist change also tend to be divided into two distinct groups. About half, or roughly 8 percent, are those who simply want to work in an uncomplicated world, doing what they know and that with which they are comfortable. Often they have invested much time in perfecting their skills and, no matter the logic, don't want to change. They are insecure, don't see the need or are uninterested in change at this point in their lives. Some have been singed so often by repetitive and valueless changes that they are burnt out. Often these men and women are the ones whose bodies are at work while their minds are elsewhere. We had lots of these people in the Canadian Forces and National Defence, many of whom used the expression, "If it ain't broke, don't fix it." But many of them avoided change because they were what Walter Natynczyk, now Chief of the Defence Staff, used to describe, using an American military term, as "ROAD: Retired on Active Duty."

It doesn't matter what you do with this 8 percent; you won't change them. But it really does not matter—they can continue to do very good things for you. Those good things are what I describe as "doing routine things routinely." In every organization those routine things must be done, whether it's maintaining buildings, ordering supplies, ensuring adherence to regulations such as fire and safety or countless other tasks. In our organizations, we tried to become so efficient that a maximum of 40 percent of our time was required for it. That way, 60 percent of our time was available to make ourselves competitive, get the change right, build the right consortia and win the war for talent. I liken it to a fighter plane: the plane is designed so that the pilot is required to spend not more than 40 percent of his time and focus flying the machine and therefore has available at least 60 percent of his time and focus to use the onboard systems to fight, which is why the plane was developed and carries awesome weapons. These 8 percent or so of people can "fly the plane," do the routine things routinely, develop constant expertise to get even better at it and help the company function. They are the reason you can fight. They are not the danger and certainly are not the ones to say farewell to in a downturn.

The other half of the 15 percent who resist change *is* a danger. They are a danger to the company and to your leadership. They are the ones to set free during downturns or, really, at the first opportunity. Those roughly 7 percent resist change because in most cases they have their own view of what needs to be done for the company and it does not accord with yours. They view themselves as hard done by, bypassed leaders who should have your job.

This small percentage consists of those angry and dissatisfied people who use their energy to obstruct, delay and avoid all the things you need done to move forward. I encountered one of them in a unit I commanded. He was a non-commissioned officer who felt that after being in the unit for several months he had learned all there was to know. He considered commanding a fighting vehicle beneath him, believed that the only job worthy of him in the unit was mine (that of commanding officer), which he felt he could do much better than me. His caustic, energy-sapping attitude was corrosive to all of us, and within weeks we helped him find a new profession. Identifying and removing these soul-sucking, energy-absorbing and ulcer-causing people from your company is essential. It is perhaps of even greater importance than identifying, recruiting or reinforcing the 8 percent who are visionaries at the other end of the curve.

In the Canadian Forces, a good chunk of the 7 percent in this group of change resisters were what we often referred to as "iron majors." That is, officers who had been given the opportunity to learn and show their capability and potential as captains or majors and had failed to do so to the level that others had. Their careers had peaked at the rank of major, and there they remained, for upward of twenty years, in staff jobs that filled the buildings in Ottawa or other major headquarters. Experts in the process, often *owners* of the process, they can delay, obfuscate, or cause to fail even the wisest change initiative that does not correspond with their view. During endless coffee and smoke breaks, they become convinced that they should be in charge of the entire operation.

As Chief of the Defence Staff, I believed that the solution to the insecurity or cynicism that countered the Canadian Forces'

153

overwhelming need to change was to present radical evidence. That is, to effect radical change, our men and women needed to see strong evidence of why the change was necessary and, further, why this particular change was what was right. The line of logic had to be solid, visible and communicated strongly so that the thread that linked the change back to the cause was clear to all.

Let me give you just one example. The Canadian Forces had to make some changes in its physical fitness standards, having lost the focus on fitness somewhat over the previous twenty years. Uniformed men and women needed to be fitter to do the job, and that meant we had to institute a new standard, and we had to help and encourage people to achieve it. This was a positive approach but still was a radical change, as those who could not meet the expectations after a period of preparation would find their career options limited, with no courses to prepare them for the next rank, no operational postings to round out their experience and thus their potential release looming.

We started showing around a picture of Canadian troops in Afghanistan: what they were doing, what they had to wear to do that and what this meant in practical terms. In the photo, the soldier wears boots, kneepads and uniform; a Kevlar helmet; a bracket for night-vision goggles and protective glasses; a personal role radio; a flack vest (Kevlar and steel plates); a load-carrying vest with numerous pockets filled with ammunition, grenades and tools, among other things; a hydration system with a gallon of water; an automatic weapon; a pistol plus ammunition; a rocket launcher; and four missiles. I would point out that the soldier was wearing or carrying 110 pounds, in fifty-three-degree Celsius heat, and that someone started shooting at him and his buddies only thirty seconds after the photo had been taken.

Our men and women from the air, land and sea were serving there, and each had to meet the same demands. If you were not fit, you could not do this; you would not be successful at your mission. You'd be more likely to die, and if you died, your buddies were more likely to be wounded or die. All of which was unacceptable. Nobody questioned the need for new physical fitness standards.

CHAPTER 21

ACTION TALKS, BS WALKS

If all the meetings and discussions in Ottawa ever resulted in anything actually happening, Canada would be the world's superpower. We would have the strongest economy in the world and be able to shape the development of it in accordance with our interests and our values, single-handedly. But of course, they don't and we can't.

As a leader, you learn to recognize that there are talkers and there are doers. When I was Chief of the Defence Staff, I had the opportunity to speak frequently, usually at length, to large numbers of people within the Canadian Forces and the public service and to Canadians across the nation. It was a pleasure to spend time explaining the challenges the Forces faced, the proposed solution for each of them, what our long-term effect would be and what their part in it was, and to articulate the pride that we all could feel. I'm sure it had some effect, but that effect was minuscule when compared to concrete actions.

I talked a lot about values: honesty, loyalty, hard work and respect. But naming these values isn't the same as showing them. How does one *see* the abstract concepts of which I spoke? And the people in uniform, their families and the civilians who supported them had all heard the words before. The word "transformation," for example, had been used so often without any visible change (except perhaps negative) that it had lost its credibility and power to inspire. Men and women simply no longer believed the words their leaders said and, indeed, waited for proof that it was all just talk once again. Reorganizations had taken place, people had been promoted, removed and regrouped, and task loads increased time after time after time. We used to joke, when the Warsaw Pact was still around, that the KGB had a special room in their dungeons where they tortured political prisoners by sliding under the door, each month, the latest organizational chart of the Canadian Forces. It would be sure to drive them to submit guilty pleas no matter what the charges.

Despite all the talk, nothing had ever really seemed to change, and what change there was did not appear to be for the better. The equipment became older and there was less of it, training continued to be reduced or cut completely and units became ghosts of their officially approved strengths. As missions kept coming, many in the Forces starting looking at the world with the "thousand yard stare" of the combat-fatigued. Actions had not matched the words, and people truly did lose faith, both in their leaders and their country.

I knew that unless I wanted to be perceived as a two-faced liar by those I led, my actions and values had to match: my actions had to become the articulation of my values. I had to live my values. Although people couldn't see the abstract concepts I spoke about, what they *could* see were my actions and the actions of the rest of the leadership in the Canadian Forces and the Canadian government. We faced this challenge squarely, which was why I was so insistent when I was interviewed for the job of Chief of the Defence Staff by the minister of national defence, Bill Graham, and the prime minister, Paul Martin, that money and political decisions had to come with the appointment. Along with the announcement that I would be the new chief would have to come more funding and a new defence policy. Turning that task into reality took a bit longer than anyone wanted, but we did get it done. The action with perhaps the greatest splash was the purchase of the C-17 Globemaster strategic lift airplanes.

Gordon O'Connor, who took over as minister of national defence when the Conservatives took power, deserves full credit for this. He and I had differing opinions on which priority had to be executed first. We launched several simultaneously, and that of the C-17 was the first to come to fruition. Signing a contract for four of these big aircraft in February 2007, with the delivery of the first aircraft slated for 9 August 2007, was an incredible accomplishment and immediately revolutionized how the Canadian Forces could do business. The eyes of men and women in uniform opened wide with the arrival of the first plane, and I began to hear comments like "My God, they're serious. They actually are going to change the CF" from every part of the force. The "they" was us, the senior leaders of government and the Canadian Forces. Our actions had spoken loudly and made believers of thousands of skeptics.

Even more became believers when, just two days after the initial aircraft landed in Abbotsford, British Columbia—the first time a Canadian-flagged C-17 had landed in Canada—it was off on its first mission, delivering a massive load of humanitarian assistance to Jamaica, which had just been hit by a deadly tropical storm. Others, perhaps still not convinced the positive change was real (after all, we'd had decades where promises came to nothing), were converted when two days after returning from Jamaica the same plane ran a resupply mission to Kandahar, carrying huge quantities of ammunition that our men and women desperately needed in the fight against the Taliban. Never mind that the aircraft captain was an American officer, on loan from the US Air Force to help us bring the fleet into service; it was action. Bringing the remaining three aircraft into service over the next six months convinced even those few disbelievers left that the change was, after all this time, serious.

It wasn't just the air force, or that aircraft, however, that gave weight to the changes we were making in the military; it was all of the other changes going on at the same time as well. Four planes, no matter how great an asset, did not a transformed Canadian Forces make. It took the concerted and continuous action of rapidly delivering tanks to Afghanistan when our troops said they needed them following Operation Medusa in late summer 2006. It included but was not restricted to delivery of a new, towed artillery piece, the world's best, called the M777 howitzer. Extremely accurate, even with normal "dumb" artillery shells, this powerful, long-barreled gun was also capable of firing munitions that could fly through the window of a house if that's where we wanted them to go. I used to joke with the gunners that every time they used one of the guided shells, it was the equivalent of firing a brand-new Ferrari downrange, and they had better make sure the target was worth the cost.

Each subsequent action, from signing contracts for new C130J tactical transport aircraft (the first of which landed in Trenton, Ontario, on 4 June 2010) and Chinook helicopters, to leasing long-range and hugely useful UAVs (unmanned aerial vehicles) for Afghanistan, to restoration of the Aurora maritime surveillance aircraft and acceptance of training and harbour patrol boats by the navy, to a contract for an immediate multi-billion-dollar upgrade of our Halifax-class warships were all part of convincing people, by our actions, that we would rebuild the Canadian military. Again, our actions spoke loudly.

Those large and essential actions were crucial, but so were the smaller actions that demonstrated that our men and women were valued and that made them and their families feel appreciated, not just by their leaders but by all Canadians. Welcoming returning soldiers, sailors, airmen and airwomen back to Canada; thanking them for their work internationally and for sharing the risks in places like Afghanistan; presenting some man, woman or child a Chief of the Defence Staff award for incredible performance, and doing this in front of their peers and colleagues all spoke to the values we held dear.

It wasn't just me who did it. Our leaders at every level, from the Governor General to the prime minister to the most recently promoted section commander, believed in *doing* things, after appropriate thought and discussion, as opposed to endlessly *talking* about doing things—so common in the political world.

The impact was enormous, powerful and wonderful to watch. Our values were clear and our actions were so loud that no one could miss hearing them.

There is a time to talk and a time to do. As a leader, if you want to get a brick wall built, sometimes you have to pick up the first brick and demonstrate, by your actions, that you're going to build it.

CHAPTER 22

TRAIN HARD, FIGHT EASY

There are many reasons to invest in training and preparing both yourself and those who follow you. Obviously, you can prepare people to do a specific job, which is certainly much easier to do if that job involves a skill set easily adaptable to classroom or simulator. Practising sequences, responses, trouble shooting and changing parts are all easy and immensely cheaper than learning on the job, where errors can be expensive. A few lessons, a bit of training, some constructive criticism and then the opportunity to try again is extremely valuable, and directly and positively affects your bottom line, no matter how you define it.

The most difficult challenge in training, but the one with the most incredible return, is training and educating people in a group. Training leaders to lead, the mind to think, particularly when stressed, and building a leadership team based on implementing a common vision can be both frustrating and powerful. The effort can differentiate you from your competitors in a way that even you might not realize until later. General Sir Michael Jackson, former Chief of the General Staff, British Army, used to say that the land battles successfully fought in Iraq in 2003 by the British Forces were actually won on the training grounds of Suffield, Alberta, where for years the Brits have focused on collective training—building teams with leaders who operate seamlessly. I'm not sure that, in the middle of long days and nights of repetitive events, anyone participating in the Suffield training would have predicted it would make the difference when facing Saddam Hussein's Republican Guard, but it did.

163

We in Canada could probably say something similar: that Operation Medusa, fought in late summer and early fall 2006 against a determined and numerous Taliban foe intent on taking or at least isolating Kandahar City, was a success because of the training that took place in the Canadian Manoeuvre Training Centre in Wainwright, Alberta. We built the teams, including the leadership teams, which in the words of the minister of defence for Afghanistan, General Rahim Wardak, prevented the fall of the Afghan government in Kabul and the resulting descent of Afghanistan, and perhaps the rest of Southwest Asia, into chaos.

One of the great challenges in collective training, and we faced this regularly in Ottawa, was getting the time and involvement of senior leaders, either appointed or elected. This was important when we were running both planning and exercise scenarios for a Canadian response to various disasters that might or might not occur, particularly here at home where Canadians live and work.

One of the things that had stuck in my mind back in the 1980s was a comment by a British special forces officer who, when describing the very realistic exercises the British Forces ran to be as ready as possible for national contingencies, said, "When we play, Maggie [Thatcher] plays." We never did see that in Canada. Sadly, instead of senior government leaders, a delegation would come to represent them and their department. Thus, when things went critical during a terrorist attack, for example, the weak link in how we updated our information, evaluated the threat, considered options, made recommendations and then, in particular, requested certain decisions would be the senior leader with the responsibility to do so. This would be especially obvious, for example, in a decision on what action to take if an aircraft were hijacked and going to be used for an attack like those on 11 September 2001. When doing all the things I just described and making recommendations that might end the lives of hundreds of innocent folks on that aircraft, it would have been nice to believe that the thought process to arrive at such a decision had been thoroughly practised.

A thoroughly practised thought process was particularly important if the "flash to bang time," as I called it, was only minutes. That is to say, if there were only minutes from the first indications that something was wrong to the need to make a decision. We needed to reach key people quickly, and the fact that we would often be doing this over the phone made the need for training obvious.

Training to prepare for not only the most difficult events but also for getting the routine things done routinely, and improving by incorporating lessons learned, is important, but it is equally important for you, the leader, to get out and "play" with your followers. Join them in the training seminars or workshops and dive into the learning process alongside them. I was heartened, upon leaving the Canadian Forces, to see that when Ed Clark brought together people from the TD Bank Financial Group team for either a day or a several-day event, he too was there. He brought his personal touch but, much more important, his presence signalled that he considered the development opportunity important. Likewise, when I attended several sessions of Telus leaders brought together for a week to continue their development, Darren Entwistle, president and CEO, was there, demonstrating by his presence and participation that the sessions were important.

There are many reasons why you, as a leader, have to train yourself, participate in training your team and understand and influence how the overall training and mentoring of every single man and woman in your organization takes place. This is not the responsibility of Human Resources (a term I think demeans the very humanness of good men and women everywhere who give their all for you). This is leaders' business and you must tend to it.

Reason number one why you should pay attention is because of the work done by Carol McCann and Ross Pigeau for the Canadian Forces as part of the study of command and leadership. They define two types of leadership: explicit and implicit. An "explicit leadership" is one in which a leader has to constantly give detailed direction and guidance and to very closely supervise all activities because the people following that leader either do not fully understand what they are trying to achieve or do not know how they are going to achieve it, even if they understand what the goal is. Absence of the leader, in this scenario, means a diminution of the work being done because people wait around to be told what to do, which results in insecurity and, usually, many mistakes. This type of situation often occurs in new units where people don't know each other, following changes of leadership or, frighteningly, if the leader has tried to focus on other tools rather than on building that network of people. Explicit leadership leans toward encouraging people to bring their bodies but not their minds to work and to wait to be told exactly what to do.

This leadership style is contrasted against "implicit leadership," in which the vision, or what the group or organization is trying to achieve, is a clear, common goal understood by all. Additionally, those being led are comfortable with the goal and understand well how the leader intends to achieve that vision (the strategy), what his or her guidelines and values are and what their own role in that strategy is. They have a common vision and an implicit understanding of what it will take to implement that vision and get going to do it. They have accepted a role and responsibilities, they bring their bodies and minds to work, they don't need detailed direction or supervision to get things done right and they themselves extract a satisfaction from working toward the goal, knowing that it is all worthwhile. It is somewhat like having clones of the leader, but that is not how I would describe it.

Many people, in fact, said to me as we launched down the road of transforming the Canadian Forces and doing all the things we needed to do, "Sir, you need a thousand clones." My response was always the same. I didn't need a thousand clones because, first, I didn't want everyone around me thinking exactly like me. That could be dangerous and could lead to overlooking critical options and opportunities. Instead, I wanted people assimilating and sharing our common vision for the CF and the values with which we would achieve it, understanding the general strategy to implement that vision, learning from my guidance, helping to build the road to practically get the many, many tasks done and bringing their bodies and minds in the application of our great mission. I wanted those thousands of talented men and women in the CF and DND putting their fertile imaginations, initiative, experience, education, training and enthusiasm to work every day. That's why I did not want a thousand clones, and that's why a common vision and implicit leadership can be so powerful: it achieves all of that.

"Second," I would say, "instead of a thousand clones, we have something much better. We have so many of us who already had that common vision and implicit leadership because of our training and development." Many of us had trained together; worked together on operations and as part of staff for years; argued with each other over vision, strategy and tactics (watch fighter pilots talk with their hands at the bar if you want to observe the intensity of those discussions); been brutally grounded by others when our beliefs were not based on common sense; had the occasional "pop" to lubricate those discussions; and were in each others' minds, so to speak, to an extent unheard of in any other profession. We had already largely achieved that common vision, and the step to implicit leadership from there was easy. There was little need for long directives or detailed orders, and no need to have everything clear before launching a CF transformation. Our confidence in each other was such that starting with a 60 to 70 percent solution was normal; we'd sort the other, remaining stuff out along the way.

The confidence, inclusiveness, boldness and initiative that follows from building to a common vision and, with that common vision as the base, the development of such an incredibly close team that implicit leadership is the norm gets multiplied thousands of times because people feel part of what is being done, feel valued and want to contribute. They will give you both their bodies and minds, and you cannot beat that.

Training helps develop this part of the leadership superbly and prevents having to learn many painful lessons on the job. When I was a tank squadron commander in the Royal Canadian Dragoons back in the mid-1980s, forward stationed in West Germany with our Canadian brigade, I had the opportunity to learn this directly—though I didn't realize it at the time (almost twenty years later, Carol McCann and Ross Pigeau described it for me). In the squadron of 120 fine Canadian soldiers (all men in those days), we had nineteen fighting main battle tanks, commanded by nineteen people, including me. The other eighteen were a healthy mix of young officers, seasoned non-commissioned officers and junior leaders on their first leadership appointment. We had a training day a week. The most valuable tool in that training was a sand table, a box about twelve feet long and six feet wide filled with sand, which we could turn into a replica of various regions—flat and open, wooded, hilly, wet or anything else.

The tank commanders, each having a tactical role in the squadron, sat around the table with me, their commander, at one end. In the sand we had placed model tanks, replicas of woods, buildings, bridges and, of course, the enemy. Someone would set up a scenario, one that started out easy but got progressively more difficult, and we would commence a typical operation, such as a mission to advance and secure a hill. The enemy would engage us and we would have to respond. We had been taught a simple process for reacting, using drills we all knew, so that damage and losses would be minimized. We worked then to develop a simple process to analyze the problem, determine a solution, develop a plan and execute it, all within minutes and while under fire. The plan included every asset available, from engineers to clear routes, to artillery to suppress enemy fire, to air attacks to destroy any retreating survivors. The execution meant attacking and destroying the enemy.

Using the sand table, my crew commanders and I went through scenario after scenario, day after day, building from the simplest to the very complex and difficult (as most operations are) and bringing in our sister fighting arms as we progressed. On each operation, the tank commanders went through their analysis and actions aloud, and I would do the same as their commander. In particular, we stressed *why* we were looking at something in a specific way—the logic of it. We did a hot wash, as we called it, both during the first scenarios and then after each operation, exploring what went right and why, what did not go so well and what we were going to do next time out to reinforce the positive and mitigate the negative.

Week after week, we conducted these exercises around the sand table, learning our business, developing a thorough understanding of what we had to do and, most important, learning to understand each other. We also developed a level of implicit intent in the squadron that I still remember with some awe. All of us would know when something happened what the commander would be thinking, how we could help him, what we could do to start implementing and how we could neutralize the major risks. What had taken us thirty to sixty minutes or more when we first started the training sessions was now, with minimal conversation, complete in five to ten.

The true value of this became clear later that year, in August 1986, when my combat team, now comprising some fifty fighting vehicles including our tanks, infantry, artillery, engineers, reconnaissance, specialty vehicles (at one point we had eleven enormous bridge-laying tanks attached) and about five hundred soldiers, was put through a forty-eight-hour test of its capabilities by senior headquarters. The test had all the assets and the potential necessary to mess us up completely. But we blew those trying to test us away, moving with dispatch, good tactics, imagination and remarkable cohesiveness. No matter where the enemy showed, we struck him from a flank, from the rear, before we were expected, or we bypassed him outright. Our training had paid off. We functioned as one team, and even the most junior soldier understood the part he had to play. Training works, but when you do it collectively for your leaders, it works only if you participate as fully as they do.

We had prefaced the sand table training with education and followed it with much more. The theory had been first taught to individuals, then the group. Chalk talks (using blackboard chalk to illustrate and draw things) helped put structure to the theory, and each commander had been trained to command his tank, to move it and fight it, before those sand table exercises. After the exercises, we went as a group into various local areas, without our troops and vehicles, testing our problem solving and teamwork against real terrain, as opposed to sand undulations. Lastly, we exercised with our troops and equipment at every opportunity. However, the crux of our success remained the ability to move from explicit to implicit intent, and react faster than the enemy could. In short, we were inside the enemy decision cycle. Because everybody involved was working to reach one goal, they could make decisions better and faster and so, in that forty-eight-hour test put to us by headquarters, we beat the enemy hands-down. Again, the key to that was our sand table work. The question I would ask leaders at every level was, "Where's your sand table, and what does it look like?"

I brought that philosophy of instilling shared intent with those who follow and cementing it through training to my responsibilities as Chief of the Defence Staff and ensured that it was used in every approach to meeting those responsibilities. Whether the leaders working under me literally had a table filled with sand or a computer simulation or something else, that training and practice was essential to establishing that their subordinates understood their intent so that it was implicit in everything they did.

The "teaching to think" part of training or education should not be underestimated either. Most people have never had access to such personal development, but despite the comprehensive and expensive programs for senior managers offered at higher educational and leadership institutions, it is actually quite simple to do. In the Canadian Forces, from the earliest days of preparing to be leaders, we were trained in how to think, something especially important when under stress. Considering simple battle strategy helped you formulate your thoughts, move through a problem from its appearance to solution and, through constant practice, training with others and mentoring (in those days, mentoring essentially amounted to brutal criticism), learn to use that process to move coherently from one step to the next and then onto logical options and an equally logical solution. I've reviewed several leadership programs in these last several years, from Harvard and Queen's universities and other institutions, and quickly realized that our program from thirty years ago was almost identical to theirs. What was different was the nomenclature or words used and, most certainly, the cost.

When considering the value of learning how to think, one incident in particular leaps out at me. I was in the business of commanding a combat team of tanks and all the rest of the combat arms attached to me, but in this case I was doing it in our training area in Gagetown, New Brunswick, where much of the army goes through training. I was on a practical course, learning the business for my next challenge (commanding the squadron in West Germany) and was being tested. We had appeared on a crest, astride a road entering a thickly wooded area, and were shot at by an enemy placed by our directing staff to offer the greatest challenge.

For a second I was stumped. But all the training we had undergone kicked in and my mind started, at lightning speed (or at least as close to it as my mind could work), to work through the problem: What kind of enemy was I facing and what would he do? How could we neutralize him? What surprises awaited us? How could we get at him? These questions and all of the other points that I knew I had to consider flowed quickly and logically through my mind. Yes, I still faced possible surprises from the right flank, but I knew that a smoke screen fired by the artillery could neutralize that threat if we approached from the woods, for example. Within a few minutes, while the rest of the combat team developed the situation, I had conceived a plan, allocated the appropriate resources and capabilities to each part and had communicated it with very few words over the radio net so that we could launch to a successful conclusion.

As always, there were many parts of training that contributed to being ready for the unexpected, but the core was being able to think in a structured, logical manner, incorporating the necessary factors and following those factors to commonsense deductions and then applying those deductions to the problem at hand. The coherency of the plan allowed its simple execution, both contributing factors to success.

Training is an effective way not just to prepare people to do their individual jobs but also to build a team—to shift from explicit intent where you have to guide all with detailed instructions to implicit intent where not only your vision and strategy are shared but so is much of how you would approach the problems faced each day. Yet again, the confidence, inclusiveness and boldness that follows from that gets multiplied numerous times because people feel they are a part of what is happening and thus will give you their bodies and their minds each day. You can't beat that.

173

CHAPTER 23

COMMUNICATION IS KEY

Communication based on "messaging," or any of the other sexy tools and gadgets provided by those who make millions building and selling such gadgets, will fail if that's all there is. Unless your vision is clear, your strategy to get there is well thought out, your network of people has been built and enabled and your tactics are ethical, the chances of your being able to sell your brand, to get people to believe the messages or even succeed, are minimal. If you have the meat, the rest will come.

When the Canadian Forces looked to reconnect with Canadians, we knew intuitively that several things would have massive impact. First, Canadians across the country were screaming for visible leadership, and that meant that leaders in the Canadian Forces, if they were visible, had to resonate with them and have credibility, and be able to vastly improve the connection we sought. Second, we had to build on real change, seen as common sense and which would quickly start to give us a credible base from which to reach out. Third, we had to grab attention. The opportunities to do all three abounded.

At the ceremony when I took command on 4 February 2005, I took the opportunity to get that attention, in the presence of Prime Minister Paul Martin, Governor General Adrienne Clarkson, cabinet ministers, senators, friends, family, the media and many uniformed men and women. After I introduced the various members of our personal, military and operational families, there was little doubt in anybody's mind that these families were important. I then acknowledged that, in our country, we in the Forces would always ask for more money than we would ever get, and we probably would never be able to give the men and women enough money to do all the jobs we asked them to do, but we could give them too little and that is what we were then doing. I asked the Government of Canada to remember us in its budgets.

The media focused on that and we got attention. There was no doubt Canadians in general took note of this, and when just a few months later I said publicly that our job in the Canadian Forces was to be able to kill people, we again had the attention we wanted. Outside the Forces, our target audience was the Canadian population, all 35 million people, and which included voters, future recruits, politicians running for re-election and the constituents who decided the politicians' views. We had their attention and, confirming my belief that our credibility with Canadians was vital, one poll indicated the Canadian Forces had become the most trusted institution in Canada, a far cry from our head-hanging days of the Somalia Affair.

The only way to be fully aware of what is happening in your company and with the people who work for you is to communicate with them and to talk to your customers and to those who can influence you negatively or positively. The communication must go both ways, and you will fail if you are always the one doing the talking. If you don't listen, you will miss the opportunity to focus on key issues because, given a chance, people will bring them up for you. You will also be quickly tuned out by whichever group you are throwing words at, becoming simply another person full of her own importance who likes to hear herself talk.

In any operational cycle, regardless of whether it's a military or a production cycle, there are invariably similar steps. People observe (learn), orient their approach to their observations, decide, act and then reassess to determine if they got it right. Communication is critical in all of the steps and begins, as we say in the army, at the beginning. Observation can take many forms, and one of those is hearing from all those around you. As you orient to the job, you learn the most from those around you, and as you make decisions, that information keeps coming. The production process is probably the greatest opportunity to learn if the lines of communication—from the top of the company to the bottom and across the horizontal levels—are good. If they are not, you'll miss much of what is critical.

Communication is essential to realize the longer-term vision, to bring people onside to the approach and to help all of you learn from everything you do and then improve or adapt to changing circumstances so you remain ahead of the competition. There are countless ways to communicate, including drawing plans, showing videos and populating social networking sites such as Facebook. Even though I believe in the many ways that communication is possible and I have used most of them over the past several years, I don't believe anything can replace the eye-to-eye method of communication. But that direct approach can be tough to establish, particularly when you work in a large organization such as the Canadian Forces and particularly when your people are scattered around the world and in some of the most inhospitable places on the planet. For us, those locations ranged from brutally cold Alert, Nunavut, to the blistering hot desert of southern Afghanistan and just about every ocean and flight path in between. Simply getting to most locations was in itself a major challenge, involving time, logistics and risk.

The challenge was worth it. Building a bond in large organizations between senior leaders and those who are relatively junior in the group is difficult. Direct communication allows you to start that process. It allows you to look the people you lead in the eye, answer their questions, joke with them, recognize them and, above all, establish your credibility with them. I found that when I had a chance to talk to people and discuss the burning issues with them, they already knew about 98 percent of what I was going to say, no matter who or where they were. They were well connected, knew where to find information and were up to speed. To our credit, the leadership of the Forces had done a pretty good job of getting the word out quickly.

As I spoke my audiences would judge me. They kept one ear tuned in just in case I said something new, but most of their focus was on how I spoke: my body language, whether I "rounded sharp corners" on sensitive issues and, most important, whether I was putting a political, or politically correct, spin on my answers to questions and problems. They were judging my worthiness and credibility, and above all, judging whether I was someone whom they wanted to invest in and follow for the immediate duration. They were deciding whether their bodies, minds or both came to work each day. It took me a few times with groups to understand that, but it was true. Each time with a group was, for me, time in the gladiator pit.

I loved laying out our approach: establishing what we were trying to achieve, where comfort in success was high, where chance of success was low and what we had to do to improve those chances. The challenge of being judged by those I led, far from making me insecure, exhilarated me. Just as I had judged my Chiefs of the Defence Staff each time I went to their seminars as a young general officer, now they were judging me and letting me know how I had done.

The youngest and most junior men and women in the service had in mind the links between tactics and strategy, not in attacking the enemy but in building a better Canadian Forces for the future. It's not the case today in the Canadian Forces that you do your job and we'll let you know if something is important and involves you. These people were connected, smart and courageous. After all, anyone who had just charged into enemy machine-gun fire had to have courage.

One example of direct and powerful communication with these young people occurred in the late spring of 2006 in Kandahar, just over a year after I had taken the appointment as Chief of the Defence Staff. We had slogged through the discussions to refine our vision and had launched a transformation of the Canadian Forces. I went to Kandahar to visit the first contingent on the ground, commanded by Brigadier-General David Fraser and built around the battle group commanded by Lieutenant-Colonel Ian Hope, 2nd Battalion, Princess Patricia's Canadian Light Infantry, from Edmonton, Alberta. After a few hours in Kandahar Airfield, from where all operations were supported, we helicoptered into Shah Wali Kot, a dusty, dirty, impoverished community north of the airbase, built on a nexus of goat trails leading to and from Kandahar City that crossed high, rock-strewn, imposing hills. Arriving on the helicopter landing zone in a cloud of dust—what our soldiers commonly refer to as "lunar dust," which is typically about fifteen centimetres deep on the ground, feels like a gritty talcum powder and gets into every-thing, and I do mean everything—we were met by our platoon of about forty.

This platoon of men and women manned a patrol base right smack in the middle of what Ian called the "rat line"—the route Taliban fighters took to Pakistan for rest, training or preparation and then again when returning to Afghanistan to kill people. The outpost, a mud-walled fort reminiscent of those occupied by the French Foreign Legion, was there to dominate that ground and interrupt the easy Taliban movement. Conditions were austere, to say the least, with hard rations for meals, an outdoor toilet built over half of an oil drum, temperatures in the high forties Celsius and no showers. Spiders, some as big as twenty centime-tres, were the permanent inhabitants of the post. There were also scorpions and the occasional snake. Machine-gun posts on the roof completed the scene. After meeting the soldiers, conducting a foot patrol into the nearest hamlet (accompanied as usual by what seemed like hundreds of inquisitive kids), eating and being given the tour of the post (which didn't take long, as it was only about fifteen metres by fifteen metres), I sat down to visit with the soldiers.

We sat around a fire pit, but notably there was no fire in it. The soldiers explained they had lit one once and the Taliban, always watching from the nearby hills, had used the flames as an aiming point for several rocket-launched grenades. Needless to say, I was happy to support the darkness-only, no-fire policy. Our discussion ranged from how the Leafs were doing (not well) and how mail to and from Canada flowed (at the speed of molasses going uphill) to the pleasures of the fort, the cunning of the Taliban, devastation of IEDs (improvised explosive devices) and, quite quickly, to the transformation of the Forces that we had announced and launched. Throughout the evening, people came and went as they changed radio watch, sentry shift or other duty. They were all engaged in the conversation, however, and superbly informed about the activities we had undertaken. They offered no shortage of opinions and recommendations to get on with what we had started and were quite simply uninterested in the obstacles that I might face in Ottawa or elsewhere as we sought to make wide-ranging and permanent changes. Their message for Ottawa was clear: Sort it out.

A least four times various junior soldiers said what amounted to "Fine, sir, we're with you on the transformation—we should have gotten there years ago and what took you (the leadership) so long to recognize what all of us have known for so long?—but what we are interested in is how you are going to ensure this continues after you are gone, so we get the Canadian Forces the way it needs to be." I admit to initially being astounded, perhaps even shocked. I was still, in my opinion, at the beginning of my job as Chief of the Defence Staff and here they were talking about what would happen when I left. Second, we had put our focus on providing the radical evidence (I talk about this in Chapter 20) to explain why we were going to change, and this they already understood. Our emphasis was somewhat out of focus, and we needed to reshape how we approached the transformation. Third, they had clearly thought this through and were concerned about the long-term effects not being implemented. (Talk about thinking long!) Fourth, they had clearly been down the road of many changes already in their short careers and did not want to go through something again that could be described as the flavour of the month or the latest business fad.

These were practical men and women, and they wanted answers. Since I was in front of them, pinned in place, and was their leader, they wanted those answers from me. I was in the gladiator pit. I bumbled through my response the first time, but by the fourth question on the same subject my thoughts were clear.

There were many things being done, I explained, including the appointment of several leaders to senior command appointments who had learned their lessons on operations in Bosnia, Cyprus, East Timor, the First Gulf War, the Persian Gulf, Somalia, Sudan and other countries in Africa and, certainly, in Afghanistan itself. They were all of similar views on what absolutely had to be done and they were going to be around for a long time. We had changed the culture of our approach, with leaders being appointed as commanders and given the necessary authority, responsibility and accountability to accomplish missions. We had already started changing our equipment acquisitions and use to facilitate all the things we wanted to do differently. Lastly, we had made organizational changes to deliver a focused approach to our missions.

My last point was the most important by far for me and, I felt, for them. "That is all good stuff to have going on," I said, "but the crucial thing to ensure that all that we are doing continues after I am gone is you. You, young and mature soldiers alike, who must stay with the Forces, continue to serve Canada and take the lessons that you learn here and on other missions, apply them yourself and demand that they be applied throughout the entire Forces. Then, when you are the senior non-commissioned officers and the senior officers, you need to continue to drive the changes and educate and train your subordinates to do likewise. You and your battle buddies will ensure the changes continue."

I thought a lot about that one opportunity in Shah Wali Kot to communicate directly to those soldiers. I had validated much of what we were trying to do, got a thumbs-up on the approach—as well as a great impression of their morale—and been inspired by their energy and dedication even in the face of very real threats to their lives. My answers about the future triggered for me many new thoughts for change and gave me some credibility in their eyes (as well as my simply being there)—not a bad return on the investment. I left Shah Wali Kot the next day re-energized for what we had to do back in Canada. Talk of the discussion that night at the outpost ricocheted around all the troops in Afghanistan and within twenty-four hours was communicated to our colleagues in Canada. It truly was the rock thrown into a calm pond, with the ripples spreading ever outward.

I had yet another lesson in communication before leaving the next day, this one about being proactive quickly and about making sure to include your own family. Sadly, while I put much energy into ensuring our military families were looked after, I sometimes did not support my own so well. This was one of those times.

Ian Hope had joined me the next morning in Shah Wali Kot and led a combat team out for a series of meetings with village elders in the area where Captain Trevor Greene had been so viciously attacked with an axe just a few days earlier. There was no way I was going to miss being with our troops for this, and so we set off. We conducted the first meeting, and as we were ready to move for the second, an IED struck, blowing off the left front wheels of our armoured vehicle. With much commotion all round, much of it around a desire to evacuate me from the combat zone, I jumped on the radio and told Ian, so everyone could hear, that I was staying. We stabilized things quickly and I almost totally forgot the incident during the rest of my visit to other patrol and forward operating bases. But I was reminded of it upon returning to Kandahar Airfield thirty-six hours later.

By then, the incident had hit the news back in Canada—the Chief of the Defence Staff had been attacked! (The newscast made the event sound much more dramatic than it had actually been.) Of course, the more the story was repeated, the more it was exaggerated. Joyce, unaware of the incident, realized something was up only when she went to work the next morning in downtown Ottawa and the first handful of people into the office all asked how I was. It seemed, at least to her, that she was the only person in Canada who didn't know what had happened. She felt, and rightly so, that she should have heard it from me if

I had been shot at (as it was put to her). Our next phone call was slightly strained, but over time, I thought she had forgotten it.

In early November 2009 I was at Canadian Forces Base Trenton, signing copies of my first book, when a young air force major came to the table, where Joyce sat with me. "Hey, sir," he said, "last time I saw you was when you were on the radio saying you were staying with the troops after the attack. We were all ready to extract you and had every aircraft imaginable overhead, from a B-52 onward to help. We were going to blow away that grid square rather than lose you."

He was really energized in his conversation, which I was enjoying until I looked over and saw Joyce's face turning red. I realized she was reliving the experience and that there would be another strained conversation between us when we got home. "For God's sake, major," I said, "I appreciate all you've done, but you're killing me here."

Lesson learned: If you are a leader in a high-profile position and get attacked, phone home immediately.

Direct communication to the ninety thousand people, regular and reserve, in our nation's uniform and to the thousands of their family members took up probably 40 percent or more of my time. It was worth it because so much was achieved. Awesome power is unlocked when people believe in common goals. The fatigue of travel, keeping current and relating to the various groups was worth it just to meet all those who served and who supported those who served. And you know what else it did? It fired me up to go back to Ottawa and take on whoever got in my way. If those young men and women could give so much, to the point of losing their lives, then so could I. All my battles were fought, whether it was government indecision, yellow journalism, parliamentary partisanship or bureaucratic power games, because of the inspiration I continued to receive when I spoke directly to those in my charge. Looking people who are in danger directly in the eye removes any of the "games" from what we did, and consequently I had precious little time for games in Ottawa.

I like town hall meetings, where you can talk to the people gathered, taking their questions, fielding their frustrations and often sharing their emotions. My first was in Ottawa, home to one of our biggest concentrations of military and civilian personnel in the country and where any cohesive view or approach was difficult to find. Torn by tribal loyalties, politics, the media and simply the diffuse locations of our people throughout the city and region and the eight-to-four mentality that often dominated in the city, it was here that the greatest energy could be found and perhaps mobilized.

Within three weeks of assuming my appointment, and following the senior leadership work in Cornwall, I hosted four town hall meetings in two days, two of them at the Hotel Lac-Leamy for those working on the Quebec side of the National Capital Region, with about eight hundred in attendance each time, and two at the Congress Centre in central Ottawa for those on the Ottawa side. At the Congress Centre more than two thousand people, both military and civilian, attended each session, which lasted close to three hours. I used pictures to try to illustrate what the new approach of the Canadian Forces leadership would be, how the vision would affect people and what we sought to achieve. I brought into my discussion, so all could see, the other parts and pieces of the Canadian Forces and the Department of National Defence and the roles they would have to play.

Exhausted yet energized after the four sessions, I felt that they had gone amazingly well. People were engaged, and their questions indicated good morale. There was an obvious desire to shape things better and a willingness to do whatever it took to deliver the right kind of Canadian Forces for Canada. That the civilians in our department were as proud to serve in their unique way as we in uniform were in ours was incredible. We finished after those two days with about six thousand fired-up, motivated and fully aware men and women. We took the town hall meetings across the country and around the world: I spoke with about seventy thousand people across the nation and around the world in just over three years, and all of them were engaged.

Even given the power of these events, the incident that I remember most fondly—for impact, enjoyment and sheer sizzle—occurred in Petawawa in the summer of 2003. I was the army commander at the time, and we were fully committed in operations all over the world. The brigade in Petawawa, the one I had commanded in the late 1990s, was responsible for sending one contingent to Afghanistan to run the Kabul Multinational Brigade for the ISAF (International Security Assistance Force) mission in Afghanistan, a second contingent to the Balkans in our continuing mission there, and then to sustain both missions and be prepared for anything back in Canada with the remaining men and women, who were few. It was a beautiful August day for the farewell ceremony in Petawawa, with more than three thousand troops on parade, more than a thousand family members present, media in place and the Lieutenant-Governor of Ontario as our guest. Along with Chief Warrant Officer Greg Lacroix, the army's senior non-commissioned officer, I inspected the troops.

When we arrived, brigade Regimental Sergeant-Major (RSM) Wayne Ford, one of the most capable men I have ever met, was on the flank and the brigade commander, Brigadier-General Peter Devlin, was in the centre, the brigade itself in a large three-sided formation around them. The centre of that square was so far away that I could barely make out shapes of individuals, let alone which individuals were standing there. As I marched to my place, I passed Wayne and in an aside said, "Parade looks great, RSM, and I almost feel sorry that I'm going to ruin it." He grinned.

After the Lieutenant-Governor and others spoke, it was announced that I would say a few words. I turned to Peter and said, "Excuse me for taking over the parade, but I'm going to bring the troops in close." Then I went to the microphone, said hello and complimented everyone on the great-looking parade. But, I said, I couldn't see those great-looking troops who were so far away, and neither could their families, and so in ten seconds I wanted to see all three thousand gathered in and around me, as close as they could get. Nobody moved for a second, not quite believing me. Then RSM Ford said, "Get moving."

The families started cheering as the troops surged into a semicircle about ten feet from me, where I could talk to them up close. I recognized long-time buddies even in the rear rank and made jokes with those who I knew could play along. I complimented a couple of soldiers who I knew had recently excelled and walked through the four or five key messages I wanted them all to remember. It was energizing for everyone present. The families loved it, and the men and women on parade felt part of the event instead of feeling like robots standing way, way out there, far removed from the speakers.

Another opportunity to communicate through action that I'll never forget presented itself on that same parade square in the spring of 2007. The contingent from Petawawa, based on the 1st Battalion, the Royal Canadian Regiment, that had fought in Operation Medusa in the late summer and early fall of 2006, had sustained the loss of a dozen soldiers from enemy action and had finally gotten everybody home. A parade was held to present all soldiers with the medals they had earned. I went with the army commander, Lieutenant-General Andy Leslie, to Petawawa to participate and, as per protocol, was asked to inspect.

Again, there were several thousand soldiers on parade, hundreds of family members in attendance, wounded soldiers who were let out of hospital just to be there and the families of each soldier who had died. I knew the family names of all the soldiers who had died, so after taking the salute from Lieutenant-Colonel Omer Lavoie, the battle group commander, I asked that the microphone be turned on. Speaking to those gathered, I asked that one person from each family who had lost a loved one accompany me on the inspection. Within seconds, they were at my side—Jackie Girouard, Charmaine Tedford and the others. As we headed around the long front rank, I could hear them behind me, sometimes sobbing, supporting and encouraging each other, but I dared not look back. My aim was simple: to communicate to the wounded families that they were going to be part of everything we did, just like those soldiers who did return. But I knew that if I looked back, I too would cry. I finished the parade and, with Andy, pinned medals on our wounded soldiers in front of the others to show them just how much we appreciated their sacrifice and that we were going to support them in their recovery and return to a full life.

So you can see that communication can take many forms to accomplish the aim. We didn't simply speak to each other. We also completely revamped the Canadian Forces website, had crews from Combat Camera—the Forces' imagery team—shoot photographs and film of every activity in the Canadian Forces and made these available to whoever wanted them, including the media. We reached out in every way possible to educate, convince, reduce ignorance and inspire.

One thing more powerful than anything we could do, however, and we realized it very quickly, was that which independent Canadians could do to showcase our great people and their service, particularly on TV and through Internet blogging, Facebook and YouTube. Rick Mercer accompanied me to Afghanistan in October 2005 and again for Christmas 2006. Rick feels he was tricked into coming on the second trip because when I phoned him in November and asked him what he was doing on Christmas Day, he immediately anticipated an invitation to the Hilliers to partake in Joyce's delicious cooking. "No, I'm not doing anything," he responded.

"Great," I said. "So you have no reason not to come and spend Christmas with the troops in the Persian Gulf and in Kandahar." Bless him, he came, had the time of his life, connected every Canadian back to our country during that very emotional season in which to be away and handled the travel and fatigue like a trouper.

Rick took the opportunity to blog continuously about his trip and attracted huge media coverage to what our best ambassadors—that is to say, our soldiers, sailors, airmen and airwomen—were doing for us. Rick followed up with shows highlighting individual parts of the Canadian Forces and their missions and, in doing so, reached quite literally millions of Canadians.

My point with all these examples is that you have to try new ways to get a message across and leave a lasting impression, and what you do depends so very much on *you*. If you are not the eloquent, silver-tongued devil that Don Cherry is, perhaps the spoken word is not where you will have maximum impact. Use whatever means you have at your disposal to give those who want to be led a chance to get to know someone who might lead them. And look like you're having fun doing it. You will be surprised at what an enormous impression it will make.

PRESENCE SPEAKS LOUDLY

Simply being around is probably the most visible means of communication available to any leader and sends an unambiguous message to those around you. The people you lead take comfort in your presence. Having you around reduces their insecurities and confirms for them in tough times that things will get better. You offer a kind of psychological security.

Knowing when and where to be seen is vital. Showing up at the critical place at the critical moment is sometimes partly luck, but with study and practice, and by being in touch with your people and demonstrating commitment, you can know where to be and when. Militarily, this often means when things have gone wrong in a fight, when the enemy is starting to achieve success and soldiers start casting glances to the rear in anticipation of a withdrawal. That's when the leader is required to stabilize the situation and reassure and reinforce his or her followers. A rout—a defeat that turns into a disaster—usually takes place when all is at its darkest. History is replete with examples of routs, but also with examples of how the sudden appearance of a leader who issues clear, confident and unequivocal direction or sets a valorous personal example can reverse the situation. Sometimes simply the leader's presence can calm the situation and reinforce resolve, helping turn defeat into overwhelming victory.

Winston Churchill, with his presence in England both personally and through radio broadcasts, steadied the United Kingdom, the British Empire and, indeed, most of the world, after the Nazi blitzkrieg swept through and ultimately conquered France. When thoughts of defeat were in everyone's minds, Churchill's unmistakable voice on the radio, his personal appearances and above all his unshakeable will to carry on turned the tide. Despite the British Army losing almost all its major equipment, suffering appalling losses of fighting men and facing an aerial bombardment of a sort that had never been experienced before, and expecting an invasion of the islands, the British, thanks to Churchill, never doubted their eventual victory. His presence allowed those who looked to him for leadership to see his ruthless determination, optimism, physical toughness and resilience, which in and of themselves communicated confidence that victory would follow those dark days as sure as night followed day. His leadership was contagious and his resolve spread throughout the population.

During the toughest of those times, however, two others also made a difference simply by being present. King George VI and Queen Elizabeth (who most of us knew in later years as the Queen Mother) refused to leave London during the Blitz, the worst of the German bombing. After several particularly horrible air raids, they toured the hardest-hit parts of London's East

End, where the working class lived and suffered, to show that they recognized the terrible challenge and shared it with those they led and therefore served. Their refusal to leave for a safer locale and the visits to sites that had already been targeted and might be struck again were inspiring. Average working people felt that if the King and Queen could tough it out, so could they.

Your presence is most vital during times of stress, but it's important at other times as well. When I was a colonel posted in the former Yugoslavia, one of our senior non-commissioned officers was charged with arranging accommodation for the Canadians who would stay in the Croatian city of Zagreb after the UN mission was dramatically downsized. I gave her my guidance and then was otherwise occupied for the day. Knowing that she had finished her assessment of a nearby hotel, I took the few free minutes I had, dropped by and found her wrapping up negotiations with the manager. She was very relieved to see me because she felt she had negotiated an incredible deal for the rooms to house the Canadian mission and was afraid of losing them to other nationalities also looking for rooms. She needed to complete the deal soon but had no idea where I was or how to contact me to be assured that she was doing the right thing and to get my approval to spend the substantial amount of money. We compared the various options, and I made the decision to take the offer at that hotel based on her recommendation. We signed the agreement within five minutes. My part in all this took not more than fifteen minutes, including drinking a cappuccino to celebrate the deal, but my presence helped crystallize the process.

There is another story that I tell frequently. One of the Taliban commanders in southern Afghanistan was a man named

GENERAL RICK HILLIER

Mullah Dadullah, a warrior who was feared even by other Taliban leaders. He truly had the hallmarks of a serial killer. He once said that he greatly respected Canadian soldiers for their fighting skills. He knew we were good, but he was also savvy enough to know something about Canadian politics and considered our political leaders in Ottawa weak. He went on to say that the Taliban were aiming their attacks at Canadian soldiers but believed that their bullets would strike the will of the politicians in Canada and cause them to withdraw from the mission.

Those comments by Dadullah rippled through the troops deployed in Kandahar. Most soldiers, with a cynical view of Ottawa, felt there was some truth to the statement and were somewhat unsettled by it. They were insecure and uncertain, which is not conducive to confident and successful operations. After all, who wanted to be the last soldier killed in Afghanistan before the politicians lost their nerve and withdrew all the others?

Prime Minister Stephen Harper visited Afghanistan, spending two full days in Kandahar where our battle group was based. His presence at that base spoke loudly to the men and women who were risking their lives every day in firefights and ambushes with the Taliban. He was telling them, through his presence, that as the head of our government he had asked them to do this job and now he was there to show them his support, his commitment and his understanding of what they were going through. Harper was saying that he would ensure they had what was needed to do their job and that he completely understood the enormity of what we in the CF had set out to do for our country and the world. Just by being there with them, Harper conveyed a willingness to share in the omnipresent risk, tolerate the inconveniences and accept the fatigue necessary to help change the world. His visit brought a confidence and stability to our men and women in uniform that I had not seen in a long time and reinforced for me just what an impact presence has. Our young soldiers did not look upon him in the narrow, partisan manner that many did back in Canada. He was not seen as a Conservative Member of Parliament, the Conservative leader or the Conservative prime minister. He was welcomed, enthusiastically, as their prime minister, the leader of our country, and was with them to share, albeit for only a little while, the direct implications of what he had asked them to do.

In every story, of course, even the saddest, there is humour to be found. In this case, I was already on my way to Afghanistan when I heard from the prime minister that he wanted to visit. I extended my stay to meet with him. We kept his plans for the visit extremely close to our chest so that the Taliban could not prepare any surprises for him—and not only because I figured my term as Chief of the Defence Staff would be a pretty short one if we lost a prime minister in Afghanistan. Only a few people in the air force, on his security team and Brigadier-General David Fraser, our commander in Kandahar, knew he was coming. However, we wanted to arrange a proper welcome for him when the C-130 Hercules carrying him from Islamabad landed, so we gathered up a selection of men and women of all ranks to meet "someone" who was coming.

I was with the soldiers and got to visit with each over a longer-than-planned period, as the plane's landing was aborted several times because of dust storms. But finally the plane touched down and taxied up to the group. The engines shut down, the door opened and down the stairs walked the prime minister of

Canada. Making a beeline for us, Harper shook our hands, joked with everyone and had his picture taken numerous times before being escorted to his first appointment. It truly was an enjoyable event and was memorable to those participating. Their prime minister, visiting with them, on mission in Afghanistan, twelve thousand kilometres from home—how cool is that?

Immediately after the prime minister departed, a young non-commissioned officer came up to me and said, "Sir, I was so excited to meet the prime minister, particularly since I've never met one before, and to meet him here, on this mission in Kandahar, was special indeed. But with all the secrecy surrounding this visit, and with not knowing who was on the plane when it landed, for some reason I thought Don Cherry was going to walk down the stairs!" I'm not sure where she got that idea, and I never did tell the prime minister what she said. Needless to say, the impact of what he had done was enormous.

FIT NO STEREOTYPES, FOLLOW NO FADS

One real trap that you will face as a leader, particularly in a formal leadership position, is surrounding yourself with yes-men: people who have the same background as you do, who think the same way you do and generally agree with all of your opinions.

Using the same thought process, without challenge, every day is dangerous and leads to mental silos (a narrowing of your viewpoint), an inability to recognize ethical challenges or confront them (look at the way so many people went along with the flow, unethical or illegal though it may have been, in the financial companies that caused the worldwide economic collapse in 2008, or BP, whose questionable ethics permitted decisions that inevitably led to the oil catastrophe in the Gulf of Mexico) and therefore an inability to consider all the appropriate options. You may inadvertently set yourself up for failure by reducing your flexibility in responding, and you may not recognize that failure when it looms ahead of you and so be unable to correct the situation. If you want your views challenged, the flow of your logic questioned and therefore your arguments built solidly, you need to include on your team those who think outside your box, those who look at the world differently than you do.

As a leader you also need to ensure that you don't allow others in your organization to become too narrowly focused. If you do, the chances are overwhelming that your organization will not attract diverse individuals with incredible talent. When you are competing ruthlessly for the decreasing number of young men and women in the Canadian population to fill the increasing numbers of jobs available, you do not want to cut out huge slices of that already small number by not being completely inclusive, and thereby not availing yourself of the immense talents that they can bring.

To me, the power of not putting your eggs in one basket is epitomized by Sergeant Allan Pogotuk of the Canadian Rangers. When I talk to Canadian Forces groups about leadership, I often say, "Now I'm going to show you a picture of a Canadian soldier." Then I display a photograph of Allan, an Inuk who lives in northern Canada and is one of our great Canadian Rangers, who serve the Canadian Forces and all of Canada from their homes and "backyards" in the Arctic. The photo of Allan was taken when he was leading one of our platoons from the south (a relative term, here meaning Ontario) on a long-range sovereignty patrol across the vast expanse of land in the north of our country. Most people don't expect the picture of the Canadian soldier to be of a proud Inuk, frost on his face. Instead, they expect to see the stereotypical image of a young Caucasian male with a crew cut, and the surprise shows on their faces.

If we had stuck to recruiting only the stereotypical soldier, the Canadian Forces and the entire country would have missed out on the character, leadership and skills of Allan and the multitudes of other Canadians who have so much to bring to any mission and to our country. Allan, who knows the North as few others do, acts as a guide, trainer and mentor to our "southern" soldiers and functions as Canada's eyes and ears across the expanse of land and the ice masses that make up the Arctic. His dignified bearing belies his small physical stature and makes him appear much taller than he actually is. He has a natural poker face if ever I saw one, and his expression tells a story of composure and confidence.

You shouldn't become the model of the kind of person you don't want in your organization, nor should you let your organization become made up of too many similar personalities. Recruit, educate, train, develop and challenge those of different mindsets, people who don't agree with everything you say, men and women of intelligence, regardless of their colour, background, language, gender, physical stature or any of the other false barriers we sometimes impose. Talent will make you and your organization successful in its long-term and tactical missions. Talented people come in many forms, and you need to have access to them all.

The urgency of doing this is compounded by Canada's rapidly shifting demographic, a pattern seen in the populations of most of the industrialized countries. Our population is aging; youth as a percentage of that population is rapidly diminishing and every organization is in a war for talent, particularly young talent. As I mention above, there are fewer and fewer young people available and more and more companies wanting them, especially the good ones. Even the most minor constraint will multiply this negative effect, keeping you from obtaining the best talent from those available. You can grade your impact as an organization by the amount of stereotyping, deliberate or inadvertent, that you do. Your talent pool can be reduced by 10 or 20 percent or more. What kind of successful organization can do that and survive in the competitive, sometimes hostile, world we inhabit?

We in the Canadian Forces recognized the challenge and addressed it as part of our Recruit the Nation strategy. Out of a population of about 35 million people in Canada, only about 7 million were of the age to be potential recruits. When you need to attract 15,000 people a year to join your organization and you are competing with every other employer in the country for them, 7 million seems like a pretty small number. By not encouraging all groups within the population to at least consider the Forces as a career option, we would have failed without a doubt. Women make up just over half the population, so not encouraging them to join us in large numbers would have meant the number of potential recruits was only roughly 4 million men. If our recruiting pitches were appealing largely to that portion of the population that is of European ancestry, we would be restricting the pool of potential talent even more. Take away those from the Indo-Canadian community, Native Canadians, and the Muslim community and all of a sudden our recruiting base was significantly south of 500,000. To get 15,000 men and women to join us each year simply would not happen, even without considering the restrictions of fitness, education and mental acuity. So simply not being proactive, not encouraging different groups to join, would see us fail. Just imagine the desperate straits the Canadian

Forces would be in if it hadn't recruited from all groups within the population.

Many leaders fall into the trap of looking for the kinds of people they think they want. Knowing of this danger is one way of combating it. Don't let yourself and those you lead be caught in this trap. In diversity you'll find a multitude of skills that can contribute to your organization, creating what we in the Forces call a "war winner" and giving your organization an advantage over the competition.

Arriving in Afghanistan, one of the things we soon learned was the power of education. Every Afghan we met (except the Taliban) believed that education was the way out of the chaos, and I left Afghanistan moved by their quiet determination to get it. Frankly, I don't remember being nearly so enthusiastic about education when I was in my early days of school as the Afghan children I encountered were. Whenever we were on patrol we were continuously surrounded by hundreds of children of all ages (out of Afghanistan's roughly 30 million people, approximately 55 percent are under fourteen years old), many of whom made the motion of scribbling on their hands. They were asking for pencils, pens and exercise books so that they could go to school. (How different from many other countries, where the kids are usually after candy!) The first child I saw do this was a beautiful little girl about three years old. I scrambled to find a pencil to give her. As soon as I handed it to her, about seventy-five other kids appeared seemingly out of nowhere, took the pencil and left her lying in the dust with a bleeding nose.

Another problem you as a leader will face is fads, which unfortunately are the cornerstone strategy of many managers, bureaucrats and others who fail to understand the basic concept of leadership, that it's all about people. We've all seen various fads come and go: Total Quality Management, casual Fridays, and a "work hard/play hard" philosophy among them. All these flavours of the month sooner or later lose steam and are abandoned, usually after an immense investment in money and time. A leader who jumps on the latest bandwagon loses precious credibility with her people. When the latest fad is rolled out, people already know that it won't work. As a leader, if you are observant and in touch with those you lead, you'll notice that people roll their eyes, fidget and can't look you in the eye. Even before you've fully described the concept, it's already been dismissed. Fads, and their almost religious adoption by some organizations, strike at the very core of a leader's responsibility to think, and act, long term. They steer you on a zigzag course that causes confusion and creates insecurity in your organization. In fact, they destroy any risk-management approach that seeks to avoid distractions to the achievement of your vision. They indicate that the vision and strategy have not been thoroughly thought through.

Think of Rene Russo's character, Molly Griswold, in the movie *Tin Cup*. Molly shows up for a golf lesson armed with every mechanical contraption money can buy. All are guaranteed to keep her head down, her eye on the ball and her wrists straight. They put her arms in the perfect position and get her to shift her weight correctly. But the gadgets prove useless because they can't account for her swing, based on her natural rhythm and her physical capabilities. For a fad to work in your organization, its vision would have to be as finely tuned as Fred Couples' perfect swing to have any effect. Fred does not need those mechanical aids. If your approach is right, you won't need the management fads either. The very fact that you want to adopt them is a good indicator that you have done something wrong along the way.

The Department of National Defence (DND) and, to a lesser extent, the Canadian Forces, fell into that trap during the 1990s when they aggressively invested in a system called Total Quality Management (TQM), which was brought into the department through the public service with the promise that it was going to right all of our wrongs. DND and the Canadian Forces spent enormous amounts of money, energy and time elaborating on all the things TQM could do for us, and poured money into seminars, workshops and study groups to convince their people to adopt it. Even more money was sunk into studying what TQM actually was, though nobody really could define it. When it was adopted, we spent untold sums and energy to make it part of our everyday life.

TQM turned out to be a total failure. The amount of money and time spent on it, considering the eventual outcome, was appalling, particularly at a time when the budgets had been slashed to the lowest levels in decades. TQM failed because we did not have the basic pieces in place—we did not know what the Government of Canada, acting for our country, wanted for us, we had no vision for the Canadian Forces (much less one for the army, navy or air force) and we had no strategy to get there. TQM could not respond to an organization that lurched one way at the behest of a government one month and another way at the behest of a new government or new brain rush a month later.

I will always remember a general officer retreat at the staff college in Toronto in late 2002 when we invited General (retired)

203

John J. "Jack" Sheehan of the United States Marine Corps to challenge the approach of the Canadian Forces and DND. Unexpectedly, he shredded in front of us the forty-page *Strategy 2020*, a highly bureaucratic and politically correct document. The response was predictable and visceral. Those who supposedly "owned" *Strategy 2020* looked quite angry, though they kept quiet as he thoroughly exposed its dramatic faults—nobody wanted to be associated with *Strategy 2020* at that point. Most of us thought of it as a useless paperweight in any case, and what he said was simply expressing out loud what almost all of us believed. *Strategy 2020* was the ultimate management document, focused on risk management through the remnants of TQM; it was unachievable and literally not worth the paper it was written on. Ultimately, it proved a diversion, and was the result of immense effort that occupied us for almost four years without producing any real effect or output.

Keeping busy, focusing on something new, ramping up excitement about a different approach and measuring the implementation of the changes that result will distract and render helpless even the most determined visionary. It will all be for nothing unless you know where you are going and select very carefully how, and what, you will execute to get there.

CHAPTER 26

RECOGNITION IS RIGHT

It's so easy to recognize people for their extraordinary efforts that I sometimes wonder why we in the Canadian Forces managed to screw it up so badly. Everyone wants to be part of something greater than themselves. They want to make the world a better place. And when they do, naturally most of us want some kind of recognition for our accomplishments.

Few people, at least from what I have seen, want that recognition simply to stroke their egos or to lord it over others or to use it to get special privileges and perks. Most of us simply want to be recognized as a visible sign that everything we are doing is appreciated. The long hours, family stress, boring meetings, late nights and fatigue are real hardships for those who do the work necessary to get things done and particularly for those who lead others to get things done. In order for folks to continue doing what they're doing, leaders have to show them some sign of appreciation.

I once wrote an article about the importance of recognition for a Canadian Forces magazine while I was stationed at Fort Hood, Texas, with the US Army. Having watched how the Americans recognize their troops (they do it so incredibly well), I wrote that our system of recognition had been designed for the 1990s. Unfortunately, I really meant the 1890s when the British Army (many of whose traditions and prejudices were inherited by the Canadian Army) only grudgingly gave out medals or awards, and then almost entirely to officers rather than the troops, who did the bulk of the fighting and dying.

We had instilled a nineteenth-century colonial mentality in our country, with an almost unbelievable antipathy to recognizing individuals for their efforts. When I was in Bosnia, a leader told me that since everyone in his unit had performed well and achieved their goals, he wouldn't be nominating anyone for an individual award. It did not take me long to convince him of the error of his ways, not just because some in his group had clearly led the way but also because some of the most junior men and women in his command had performed in such a mature fashion that they guaranteed success, often in ranks above their permanent appointments and for which they were both very junior and unprepared. In other words, they were even more deserving of recognition than almost anyone else. We did recognize individuals from the unit, to the pleasure of everybody in it, because individually or in small teams they had made an extra difference.

In my view, there are two types of recognition systems: the formal and the informal. If you are not careful, the first type can grow into a process-driven system that becomes so tedious and

unrelated to the day-to-day activities it is supposed to be rewarding that it can fail completely. The second, or informal, system of
recognition, I believe, is highly valuable if you use it right.

Informally but publicly recognizing your people in a timely
way—soon after their great work—shows a sincere appreciation
of their efforts and sacrifices in front of their peers. As Chief of
the Defence Staff, I recognized early the power of making special
reference to someone or singling someone out of the group I was
meeting with. To keep the situation light, I would try to make a
bit of a joke about their incredible efforts, then shake their hands
and present them with the Chief of the Defence Staff's coin, a
small engraved medallion that is not an official decoration but
nonetheless represents the thanks and appreciation of the head
of the Canadian Forces.

In one incident that occurred when I was at Camp Nathan
Smith, the Provincial Construction Team camp in Kandahar,
two of our soldiers were in the turret of a light armoured vehicle, a LAV III, that was blown up. The turret, with them in it,
was thrown clear of the vehicle by about fifty feet. Both survived
and were slightly the worse for wear, but they had immediately
done their drills, met their responsibilities and carried on doing
their jobs, which I thought was just incredible. So, in front of
a couple of hundred of their comrades, I presented them each
with a coin. I told them, with much laughter from their friends,
that I was awarding it to them for setting the world's record in
the long jump with a five-hundred-kilogram weight attached. I
thanked them for being so awesome and gave each a hug, and we
all applauded their incredible devotion, much to their embar-
rassment. Still, each of them seemed to stand straighter, prouder,

growing by a couple of inches, and I know that we received even more from both over the following weeks and months.

Informal recognition must come from the heart. I meant those handshakes and hugs and thanks, with or without the coin. Now, I admit that hugging the people who work for you—physically touching them—has its risks, but I think it's a minimal and worthwhile risk to take. I hugged soldiers everywhere, men and women, in uniform or in civilian dress, in operational theatres and at ceremonies at Rideau Hall, presided over by Her Excellency, the Governor General. (I even once hugged Adrienne Clarkson, who laughed as I embraced her at a farewell ceremony on Parliament Hill, when we thanked her for being such an inspirational commander-in-chief.) I believe that hugging establishes a bond so I didn't hesitate. The absurdity of letting politically correctness prevent us from doing the right thing struck me as I talked to the troops—that is, the absurdity of it being socially acceptable to give a buddy hug to a man, whereas it is frowned upon to do the same to a woman. I gave many buddy hugs, headlocks and wrist grips to hundreds of people, men and women alike. So sue me.

Timeliness of recognition is fundamentally important. Recognizing the great things that the men and women working for you have accomplished years after the fact, when they have moved on and lost contact with the people with whom they worked to achieve so much, is counterproductive. Rather than rewarding people, such actions send clear messages: your work wasn't important enough, and neither are you, for recognition to come quickly. If you don't reward people quickly, you'll have a team that feels less loyalty to you and to the organization to which all of you belong.

It's equally important to recognize people formally and with class. I admit that we had the advantage in the Canadian Forces over most organizations, with many of our award ceremonies presided over by the Governor General of Canada in the regal surroundings of Rideau Hall. It doesn't get any better than that. But we took these advantages a step further. We organized a Canadian Forces heroes ball, with the complete and enthusiastic support of Her Excellency Michaëlle Jean, inviting about thirty heroes from across the Canadian Forces, with their spouses, partners or selected guests, and hosting them in style at a gala ball held at Rideau Hall. At the end of the night, the wife of one of the young heroes remarked in awe to my wife that it had been "a fairy tale evening."

It wasn't just the Rideau Hall events that we did in style. Thanks to great leaders like Major-General Walter Semianiaw, when we presented awards such as a Mention in Dispatches, it was done in venues such as the Museum of Civilization, where we were surrounded by the rich history of our nation in a beautiful setting. The setting itself, never mind all of the ceremony's other trappings, clearly helped remind everyone present of the importance of the award, our history and achievement and our collective future opportunities.

One last important point: include family when recognizing your team. The families of our soldiers that we saw and usually met at our events were proud. I used to joke that I could spot the families in the room by their beaming faces. We fundamentally changed our approach to include those families in all the events possible.

Lest you think the Canadian Forces is my only example of how to do this well, let me tell you about TD Bank Financial

Group, which since my retirement I've had the opportunity to participate with and support in reward and recognition events. Each ceremony was, without exception, first class, and included the top leadership of TD and their families. The events were held in inspirational venues with motivational speakers as guests, with humour and, above all, in a timely fashion. Almost everyone I spoke to was overwhelmed by being recognized publicly.

Recognizing your staff can reduce employee stress, sick leave, absenteeism and disciplinary problems that will detract from your goals. We quickly realized in the Canadian Forces that appreciation was one of our best preventative weapons against post-traumatic stress, the often debilitating psychological condition that sometimes results from combat or other stressful situations. Making each of our men or women feel valued as individuals allowed each of them to accept the challenges and stresses that went with operations. It mitigated the most deadly of those stresses and allowed them to weather the storms more robustly than men and women who did not believe they were appreciated. Feeling that you are contributing (again, to something greater than you as an individual) makes you strong, gives you confidence in your skills and abilities and leaves you understanding that you as an individual can make a difference and are important. Having that feeling validated through a reward or recognition is powerful.

Being recognized confirms your value as an individual, in your innermost self, and pumps you up psychologically. That recognition, translated into appreciation, acts as a vaccine to ward off attacks of insecurity, uselessness, stress and the psychological or mental wounding that can result.

Formally recognizing your own troops in style, with class and gravitas, sends a clear message that the work and the people involved are valued and appreciated. The resulting impact, on morale, job satisfaction, personal goals and increased engagement in the organization are priceless. The body and the mind will now come to work each day, and the value of that is huge.

Recognition is so simple that it always surprises me that people screw it up so often. Don't be afraid to shake hands, throw an arm around someone's shoulder and simply say thank you. You can't go wrong.

CHAPTER 27

RETAIN FAMILIES

Lieutenant-General Angus Watt, who was Chief of the Air Staff and commander of the air force during my time as Chief of the Defence Staff, discussed with me one day the challenges, and the excitement, of attracting young Canadians to take an interest in the Canadian Forces. We needed young people to approach our recruiting centres, to join, to be successful with entry-level training and to serve a career either of specific duration or for their working life and then retire from uniformed service with honour and a sense of accomplishment.

"Sir," Angus said, "we are in a war for talent. The shrinking percentage and number of youth in our society means that all of us—business, government and military—want those same decreasing numbers of youth. Our challenges, and our investment, to reach our recruiting targets still pale in comparison to the enormous and expensive training process that will give them the skill sets they need to do the job we ask them to do. Our investment in that training would probably drop about 10 percent for each 1 percent of our existing force ready to take release or retirement who we convince to stay for another three years. Retention is that important. And our emphasis has to be on retaining the families—not just these young men and women who wear the uniform, but their families as well."

Angus was right. His belief was founded on logical analysis of the facts put into a mental strategic framework. In my first book, *A Soldier First*, and in this one too, I talk a lot about many important aspects of leadership that we in the Canadian Forces had got right over the years, but one thing we had neither recognized nor put sufficient command focus on was looking after and supporting our families. Our record was dismal. We put up with it at a time when there was no major threat and we had no lobby group to help us change it, but now the environment had changed dramatically.

In past decades, military families were considered excess baggage, and it was the serving individual who had the responsibility of ensuring they did not become a burden to the unit. We used to have a saying in the army: "If the army wanted you to have a family, we would have issued you one." Our treatment of those families followed from that.

No recognition was made for the fact that these families, who were usually not from around the base where they were living and hence had no immediate family support network, served our country also, albeit indirectly. They were the ones who endured the stress of frequent deployments for husband, wife, father and mother, and they were the ones who carried the family on their shoulders until their partner returned or, worse, did not return. Our support for them was negligible, and that had many implications, but chief among them was a growing dissatisfaction with the military, from both the serving men and women and from their families. The direct result, contrary to what we were all trying to achieve, was an ever increasing attrition rate that made a mockery of logical developmental plans. The only saving grace in the 1990s was a sputtering economy that kept many who would have left in for just a bit longer.

Several things changed all that, however, and the revolution in support of families is underway right now. The first was the transformation in global communications and the way people stay informed. Up until the 1990s, if the husband and father was away and something went wrong at home, unless it was a dire emergency threatening life, it often took weeks before that soldier learned that the kids had been sick, the wife hospitalized, the car towed to the garage or the pipes in the house frozen, and by then it was irrelevant. (I focus on men here as the vast majority in uniform were males even into the early nineties. In addition, the combat units who deployed were still almost exclusively men. The Canadian Airborne Battle Group deployed to Somalia in 1992 had no women in it, for example.) Letters, the main source of communication, often took weeks to be delivered. Phone calls were infrequent, expensive and often frustrating (try phoning home after being abroad several months and persuading your wife to say "over" to let you know that it's your turn to talk as you use a ham radio system to connect to her). The circumstances at home had no real impact on the individual soldier, sailor or airman's performance or focus while overseas because the emergency had already been resolved by the time he became aware of it.

Now, thanks to email, the Internet and cell phones, news of sick kids, a hospitalized spouse, broken car or frozen pipes can be communicated within minutes to the loved one overseas. Now the soldiers, sailors, airmen and airwomen were facing issues and concerns at home in real time, a situation that could and often did prove acute and dangerous. The family expected to be in contact with their father, mother, husband or wife overseas, and the person deployed also wanted to be in contact and to be able to help. That became an enormous risk to commanders in the field, because the result was often men and women whose focus was not "downrange"—on the important and often deadly dangerous job they were doing—but back home with their families. Even a minor lack of focus against a capable enemy can see you dead, something we clearly did not want. That is why our support for the families had to change, quickly and dramatically.

Second, the changes came about because it was the right thing to do and it was the right time to do it. The families were caught up in a dynamic of steadily increasing risks abroad and, hence, greater worry at home. We had to address family breakdowns, stress-related illness and incidents and, tragically, the negative impacts on children.

The number of initiatives to help families prepare for military life, understand the frequent deployments, meet the challenges of long separations, address the fears of children and get through the tension of hearing about casualties without names attached was only part of the strategy. Most important was the attention paid by our commanders and even politicians, most notably the Standing Committee on National Defence and Veterans Affairs (led by Senator Colin Kenny, who deserves kudos for his efforts), which held hearings at all major military bases from 1998 to 2000 and helped articulate the crushing burdens facing those who volunteer to serve their country in uniform. Military families, for the first time, also felt valued and appreciated, and believed that someone understood what they were going through or at least was willing to listen. They felt they had someone to counsel them. Military Family Resource Centres were established to help provide family support, from drop-in centres to emergency babysitting services to professional and specialized counselling. Deploying units started organizing very real and effective deployment support centres and teams for when the majority of the unit was gone. Each day, it seemed, things got better, but the key part and change remained valuing those families.

The result was immediate and tangible. Happier men and women in uniform meant that more of them wanted to stay in the Canadian Forces. Happier families, those who felt they were part of the great adventure as opposed to being viewed as excess baggage, also had a vote—a huge one—and they were increasingly interested in staying on. The most visible results of our focus on family included an increased retention rate (that is, a decreased attrition rate, losing less of the huge investment in the men and women that the Forces trained and educated), a reduced need to recruit and vastly reduced individual training costs. Perhaps even more important was the return on the enormous stake in training, mentoring, education and operational time that each person represented, and that could come only from within the Canadian Forces. We could not go out and recruit from our competition—imagine trying to persuade Taliban commanders to join the Canadian Army—and recruits from allied military forces were so few as to have little impact. We had to train our own. A brigade commander who could command efficiently during a natural disaster like the Red River Flood or conduct strategic operations in a place like Afghanistan was a twenty-year product, without shortcuts. Trying to expand by thousands the Canadian military, particularly the army, was adding enormous extra stress to the individual training system. Unless the family support had helped change the retention dynamic, we would have been completely incapable of conducting expansion and would have failed in our mission. This was core business for leaders because it was so crucial to us in being able to execute our missions. Unappreciated and unsupported families meant higher attrition, and higher attrition possibly meant we wouldn't have had anybody to do many of the jobs we needed done and so we would fail.

The unwritten but unlimited liability contract that each serviceman or -woman accepts on joining the Canadian Forces works both ways. These men and women would put their lives on the line for Canada if we met our basic responsibilities for them and their families. One-way contracts do not work, but that was pretty much what we had for decades. The same can be said of the civilian workforce, though the liability is not unlimited for most professions. If your employees are putting in long hours, sacrificing themselves and their families to do their jobs, and you are not doing everything you can to help them out in return, sooner or later you and your organization will pay the price.

Immediately, our intention to change our approach and support to families had to become clear through our actions. The leadership at every level demonstrated just what their imagination and capabilities could deliver, with thousands of coordinated initiatives to fix the situation. My contribution was the Military Families Fund, a small pool of money from which commanders could draw on in cases of emergency and justify it after the fact. It was a shot in the arm to thousands who had never recovered from the stigma of being a "dependent" without much to depend on. One regiment, the Royal Canadian Dragoons, started a project to give the children of each deploying Dragoon a teddy bear with a uniform bearing the child's name and, most important, a digital recorder in the belly. Dad or Mom could record special words, stories or simply say "Goodnight." When they were away for the six-, nine- or twelve-month tours and the child was lonely, sick, being punished or simply missing Daddy or Mommy, he or she could cuddle that bear, touch the button and be instantly comforted. All for a cost of $25. It was invaluable. The psychological boost to families came from a combination of all that we started doing for them—the direct support, dollars in the Military Families Fund, teddy bears for children and the many other initiatives—again, an effect worth a thousand times the cost of the initiative.

FEAR IS GOOD

Fear can be a tool to help both you and others focus. As detailed in many psychological and physiological studies, fear brings the boundaries of what you see closer together, creating the tunnel vision of the main threat you face or what you need to do. It slows things down and allows you to see your focal point much more clearly. The danger is that in being so focused on the main threat or that one important issue, you lose sight of what is happening right in front of you.

The right amount of fear allows you to perform better. The trick is to not be afraid of fear itself, and to understand the advantage it gives you. (The adrenalin rush alone is better than any drug, for example.) It's equally important to prevent fear from paralyzing your actions, causing you to fail. Training and experience teach you to learn how to manage fear. Worrying about failing in training can be as damaging as failing in the real-life situation.

It is obvious how fear might be a great physical motivator for soldiers on the battlefield, as well as for the officers and generals who command them, but it can motivate in the civilian world also. In 2006, when our first battle group landed in southern Afghanistan, it was based out of an enormous coalition airbase called Kandahar Airfield. The US Army had built this huge base up from the ruins of what had been Kandahar's main international airport, beginning in 2002 soon after the Taliban were chased out of power. Our soldiers found a facility that was well appointed with all the amenities, including a row of fast-food restaurants, all of them big American chains.

What they missed along the base's "boardwalk" row of shops and restaurants was a little bit of Canada in the form of a Tim Hortons. Back in Canada we had been negotiating with Tim Hortons for several months to get it to allow a franchise to open up for our troops overseas, but the talks had stalled. Then, in February 2006, one of the reporters embedded with the battle group caught wind of the scheme and called Tim Hortons headquarters in Canada to ask about it. A relatively junior spokesman in the company's public relations department threw cold water on the idea and said definitively that it was not part of the company's business plan. The story hit the newspapers the next day and was on the TV news that night, with headlines suggesting that Tim Hortons was unwilling to support our troops overseas.

The public response was immediate and overwhelmingly negative and Tim Hortons' response was quick and positive. The company was bombarded by thousands of emails and phone calls lambasting it for not going to Kandahar to support the troops. Several Internet petitions were started, calling on Tim Hortons to go to Kandahar Airfield. Some people even suggested a boycott of the chain. It had turned into a public relations nightmare for the company. After about a week of uproar in the media and on the Internet, I received a phone call from Paul House, president and then-CEO of Tim Hortons. "We surrender, General!" he said. "We will have a franchise in Kandahar to support our troops, and we are going to do this quickly."

Six months later, the first Tim Hortons franchise outside North America opened on the boardwalk in Kandahar Airfield. It instantly became a hit, not just with the Canadian soldiers who had been longing for their usual "double double" but also among the troops from the dozens of coalition nations operating in Afghanistan. Back in Canada, the Kandahar Tim Hortons franchise became a good news story for the company. Hundreds of the chain's employees volunteered to serve a tour of duty handing out coffee and doughnuts in Kandahar, and it became the basis of an advertising campaign, not to mention dozens of favourable stories in the media. It all started with a bit of fear, instigated by a looming public relations catastrophe, that helped the company's senior executives realize what they needed to do and pushed them to do it quickly.

PART 4

EXECUTION

SIMPLIFY

One of the greatest and most helpful characteristics you can have as a leader is the ability to take sophisticated and complicated situations and simplify them for those who follow you. The reason is simple: your people will now be focused on solving the problem or winning the war, as opposed to simply trying to understand what the war is.

By the time I took over as Chief of the Defence Staff, the Canadian Forces was facing a massive shift in an increasingly complex international environment, with new technology and training added into the mix. The change was complicated even for those who spent a lifetime studying these kinds of things, and many of us had done just that. But we had to boil it all down to the basics if we were going to engender a solid understanding of what we were embarking upon. We had to get people to buy into the changes and bring both their bodies and minds into play. If we were to get onboard those whose support we needed for money, acquisition and commitment, we had to simplify our explanation of what was happening and our role in it. There can be a lot of truth contained within a ten-second sound bite, and we had to simplify our vision to almost exactly that. It was my job to do this, and although it took a few tries, I believe that I got it right.

What we boiled all the complexities down to was something I called the bear-versus-the-snakes strategy. The bear represented the former Soviet Union and its allies in the Warsaw Pact that for almost forty years threatened Western society. Canada, as part of NATO, had troops deployed in Europe for decades following the Second World War to defend against that threat. Everything we did was focused on the possibility of the Russians and their allies pouring across the Iron Curtain into western Europe and possibly beyond. We had built our army, navy and air force based on the Warsaw Pact threat, and after forty years of Cold War our attitudes and approach were set in concrete.

After the fall of the Berlin Wall in 1989, however, changes came upon us one after another at a bewildering speed. Overnight, the USSR and the Warsaw Pact disappeared and along with it the threat of mass combat between the two superpowers. Self-determination, no longer constrained by the big power blocks, led to violent breakups of states around the world. Rising religious extremism brought to the fore the new threat of terrorists not tied to or controlled by any particular country. It truly was a free-for-all.

The Canadian Forces, like every other Western military, had throughout the 1990s participated in what was termed a Revolution in Military Affairs. And, like the other Western militaries, we got the focus wrong. Yes, we endlessly studied the technology and capability required to kill columns of Soviet tanks, but we didn't absorb the fact that those enemy tank columns no longer existed. We ignored, perhaps somewhat deliberately, the fact that the new threat thrived on the chaos found in failed or failing states. Afghanistan was but one example where that chaos permitted al Qaeda to hide and flourish. Sadly, even the destruction of the World Trade Center on 11 September 2001 did not serve as a wake-up call, except to a few, like the former army commander, Lieutenant-General Mike Jeffery, my boss at the time. His ability to understand the strategic shift energized my thought process and led to the Forces' transformation.

Articulating the change was as simple as saying—and in my case also drawing—"bear to snakes." The bear, as I mentioned, was the former Soviet Union; the snakes I described as the chaos, ignorance and poverty in failed or failing states, which terrorists, and those who support them, feed upon. Pandemics start, refugees are driven out of their homes, and unless someone stems the tide of chaos, ignorance and poverty, it eventually spreads to affect neighbouring nations or even countries on the opposite side of the globe. We had always shaped ourselves for the conventional fight against the bear and were prepared to shift to combat the snakes when need arose, what we referred to as an asymmetrical threat. Now it was time to organize ourselves differently, against the snakes, since that was the conventional threat for the foreseeable future, and to be prepared to shift to combat massed tank threats or the like if they should ever arise—the symmetrical threat. The diagram made it simple and "bear to snakes" became the watchwords for transformation. It was simple and conveyed many images to describe both the threat (heavy, lumbering and largely constrained by Geneva Conventions changing to hidden, anywhere and unconstrained by anything) and how we wanted to be (heavy and lumbering changing to agile, flexible, surgical and building). People got it, and instead of wasting time and energy trying to understand the strategic approach, put that time and effort to work to figure out how to change the tactical approaches to be effective at the new strategy. "Bear to snakes" also described the change we would bring to core military jobs, but no job, no mission in the world, was any longer pure military—if it ever had been.

It's pointless to kill the leaders of insurgent groups trying to destabilize a country if you cannot at the same time help the people of that country to build a government that can run it—a government that can develop a strong economy, provide jobs and security in the real sense and encompass education, health, law and all things related to survival. Our core military tasks had to be wrapped into what I viewed as a Team Canada approach, taking stability to places abroad before that instability came to Canada. Once our core transformation was understood, that part was easy to explain; how the Canadian Forces would be part of a team made up of all parts of our society, not just government departments but business and industry as well, and would work together on Canada's behalf to achieve great things.

Most easily understood but perhaps most difficult to implement because it tackled the most entrenched remnants of the Cold War focus, was the strategy of treating Canada as an operational theatre. Our soldiers understood this, but those who viewed themselves as defenders of systems and services were reluctant to make the necessary changes, even when they saw the need to do so. Canada as an operational theatre meant, for example, that one commander, reporting directly to the Chief of the

Defence Staff, would have absolute use and therefore control of all military forces in Canada—effectively, one dog for the Chief to kick. That commander in turn would have six commanders across the country who would focus on the six distinct regions in a similar manner. The army, navy and air force commands still had to generate the forces, but those forces were not theirs to command in Canada. This made life interesting whenever I had the chance to even think about being bored.

Again, once the bear-to-snakes analogy caught on, understanding the rest was easy and led to the young soldiers in Shah Wali Kot, Afghanistan, thinking past the immediate problems (even if the immediate problem was a Taliban fighter trying to kill them) to the long-term success of what we were trying to do. Your job as leader is to simplify, and the more complex things are, the greater your responsibility to simplify.

CHAPTER 30

NO PLAN IS PERFECT,
SO EXECUTE EARLY

Executing early means you are taking advantage of momentum and opportunity to make enormous progress quickly, really a positive application of the "shock and awe" campaign of Donald Rumsfeld during the Gulf War. It also avoids a huge waste of resources and time by not working fruitlessly to seek the perfect and absolutely complete plan. My rule of thumb was to be ready to start execution with only the framework of a plan if necessary and flesh out the rest of that plan on the move. What I found was that this allowed early actions, permitted us to determine and control the momentum somewhat and, remembering that actions speak loudly, gave supporters and doubters alike visible indication of our intentions.

There was a bit more to it than that, however, and it had to do with the amount of time and work needed to complete any operation. First, any plan could be brought to somewhere around 70 percent completion very, very quickly—if not in a few hours of hard work, then at most in a couple of days. Going from about 70 percent completion to 100 percent completion, however, demanded much, much more. My experience was that the last 20 to 30 percent of any plan took many times more time and resources than the first 70 percent, and sometimes those final tasks were impossible to complete. If people need a way to assuage their insecurities, they can find it in the details and quibble about them forever. In the meantime, they lose momentum, skeptics can arm themselves and the opportunity is wasted. Without aggressive and early execution, risk reduction turns into risk aversion through that quibbling about detail. Catering to everyone on everything is simply not possible. You can't ever have all the answers, and in a risk-adverse environment, the search for those answers never ends. In our case, I was comfortable that we had the leadership team in place to get things done quickly and would not lose the opportunity afforded us.

One of the things that made up for a plan that was constantly under development was aggressive execution. Our special forces, particularly, excelled at this, following the mantra, "When in doubt, empty the magazine." Sometimes that was literally what they did. These men understood that even the best and most thorough planning and preparation rapidly reaches its best-before date and that any more time spent on it takes away from actually conducting the operation. A delay in filling in all the details increases the chances of compromised security, allowing the enemy to escape or increasing risk to friendly forces. Therefore, once comfortable that they had the best plan and preparation possible, they launched as soon as they could.

Don't wait for a complete and perfect plan that will never come together. Just get started, and let your actions speak for you.

CHAPTER 31

THINK BIG, AND GET THE BIG THINGS RIGHT

If you want to accomplish something earthshaking, do the big things first. The little things will follow, though they may take a bit more time. This principle was reinforced for me just before Christmas 2006, when I hosted a round of town hall meetings in Ottawa and discussed, among other things, how we could better support families. At one meeting, I told of a dinner party that Joyce and I hosted along with the senior airman in the Canadian Forces, Chief Warrant Officer Danny Gilbert, and his wife, Danielle, at our home. The party was a lot of fun (though it was a heck of a lot of work too), and we raised $2,000 for the Military Family Resource Centres. But I compared that to another dinner I attended where $100,000 had been raised for another cause, and I wondered aloud if we could raise even more money by having a fundraising dinner for our families who occasionally needed our help. I asked if there was anyone at the meeting who could help me.

There were many volunteers, and Lieutenant-Colonel Rodney Ward, a pilot then on staff in Ottawa, took the lead. "My view," I said, "was that we could have a major dinner in Ottawa, inviting a lot of people who want to support, particularly people with money. Joyce and I, along with Danny and Danielle, can host and we can get a big donation for the Military Family Resource Centres and start to change what we actually can do to support. Can you look at that?"

Rodney was way ahead of me. Several weeks later, he and the team of volunteers came to see me. "Forget the standalone dinner," Rodney said. "Establish a Chief of the Defence Staff's Military Families Fund and really make a difference, over the longer term, in how we help families. The country is ready for it, and it fits the Recruit the Nation strategy. We already have people like Dave Smith from Ottawa, Max Keeping from CTV, retired lieutenant-general Bill Leach and the Ottawa Senators Foundation with Dave Ready, who all want to be involved and support. What do you think?" I had been thinking within a narrow and tight lane and had therefore missed the big picture. I was embarrassed, really, because Rodney was thinking big. The Military Families Fund was launched as a result, in April 2007.

I was thinking a lot about Rodney's vision on 10 November 2009 when I attended the True Patriot Love Dinner, the brainchild of Shawn Francis, in Toronto. The prime minister, the Lieutenant-Governor and the premier of Ontario, along with two thousand other Canadians, attended the dinner and succeeded in raising almost $2 million for the Military Families Fund. Military families cried when the fund was launched because of the appreciation it showed. Rodney Ward, by thinking big, had changed the course of how a country views the families of those who serve and, consequent to that, how those families are supported and valued.

In February 2010, I was at the Canadian War Museum for the launch of the tenth anniversary of the Motorcycle Ride for Dad, with the monies raised split between prostate cancer education and the Military Families Fund. At the launch was a young soldier, looking superb in his uniform, with his lovely wife and five-month-old son, telling the story of how he and his wife, living in Petawawa, had to spend the first four months of their son's life in Ottawa because of the multiple heart surgeries the little boy had to endure. He spoke of finding the cheapest hotel, and of smuggling a microwave into the room so they could heat up food because they had no money to eat at a restaurant. They were almost at wit's end when the Military Families Fund stepped up and supported the family. The couple will be eternally grateful, even as they continue to serve our country, and a young man, with his family supported, can focus on serving his country, to our benefit, without distractions. It's truly a win-win.

Thinking big is so related to vision and thinking long that I had every right to be embarrassed for not having thought of the Military Families Fund myself. Thinking big captures people's imaginations, as it certainly did in this case, and becomes one of the major interchanges on the road to achieving your great vision. Ask yourself at every opportunity, is there a big moment here, and if so what is it?

Lieutenant-General Mike Jeffery used to say that if you have a bunch of big rocks and a lot of little ones and you have to put them all into a jar, you'll always put the big ones in first. The little ones will then naturally fall into and fill the spaces among the big ones. It doesn't work the other way around. Concentrate on the big things and the little things will take care of themselves.

BEG FORGIVENESS

If I had needed permission for everything I ever did during my long career in the Canadian Forces, not one single thing would have gotten done. Permission was a given, at least in my view, to get on with things. First, Prime Minister Paul Martin offered me the appointment of Chief of the Defence Staff knowing what I needed to do the job right. The budget of February 2005 put actions to some of the words the PM had said when giving me his guidance on rebuilding the CF by allocating significant amounts of money for specific programs that I thought the Canadian Forces urgently needed. And the defence policy paper that outlined Canada's approach to security, with an emphasis on failed and failing states, increasing security at home and building solid relationships with the United States and NATO gave us clear direction as well.

We surely didn't need any further permission to get things rolling. Our job was to implement that new strategy, and my approach was simple: we had been ordered to do something and we were going to do it. I regularly ensured that the minister of national defence was fully aware and comfortable with all we were doing, although we were not asking his permission to do anything. There is a tendency in large organizations, private and public, to stop tasks from ever getting underway by first approving the strategic direction and then forcing a separate approval for each action. To me, this dulls your competitive edge.

My job as leader was to lead, so we went ahead and just did what needed doing. Whenever anyone suggested that he or she should have been consulted on my decisions, regardless of whether that person brought anything to the fray, I simply asked forgiveness and carried on. Usually we were so far into a project that whoever had considered themselves insulted for not being asked first (and some people do go out of their way to put themselves in a position where they can be affronted) could say little, and I would just tug my forelock to show how sorry I was.

One issue I had to deal with was danger pay for our wounded soldiers who had been evacuated from a dangerous area. On dangerous missions, servicemen and -women get additional pay, or "extra allowances," for the extra risk they incur. The level of risk varies depending on the mission; the highest risk I've experienced was clearly the mission in Afghanistan. Members of the Canadian Forces get a risk allowance only when they are in direct risk to themselves, that is, at immediate risk of injury or death. Some soldiers, who had been wounded very early in their six-month tour of duty, were evacuated from theatre to be treated and to recover in Canada, and, as they were no longer in the danger zone, they lost the allowance. For our younger soldiers, the extra allowance represented a serious boost in their pay. The senior leadership and I were unaware that the wounded soldiers back in Canada weren't getting the extra, much-needed pay and how adversely it was affecting the troops. I was in Toronto when the story hit the news. Several of our soldiers who had recently returned to Canada from Afghanistan had taken it up with the media. They felt they had not been treated fairly, that they had been badly served. Getting wounded—and having the allowance cut off—had cost them as much as $15,000, tax-free. Several parents of soldiers had taken up the fight on behalf of their loved ones.

I was at a variety of events, with media in attendance, when this became the lead news item. After a quick call with the Chief of Military Personnel to confirm the facts, it became pretty clear to me what had to be done. With support for the Canadian Forces swelling across the country, no Canadian was going to find it acceptable that someone who had taken a bullet for us, was blown up or torn apart by shrapnel would suffer for his or her courage by being hit with a financial penalty. Our policy was wrong, and I had worked together with Minister of National Defence Gordon O'Connor and Stephen Harper long enough to believe that they would also consider it wrong. The morning the story hit, I was interviewed by Beverly Thomson on CTV's *Canada AM*. She began, "Yesterday, a wounded soldier said—"

I didn't even let her finish. "I've heard about it. We have a problem and we are going to fix that problem. It is not right that those Canadians should be further 'wounded' by losing money they might have earned had they cowered in a ditch, and we're going to make sure they get it. We'll need a couple of weeks to figure this out, but we are going to fix it. And, by the way, I know I have the support of the prime minister and minister of defence in this."

I repeated this same speech in about twenty more interviews over the course of the day. Having stated my thoughts publicly, there was no doubt in my mind that I would now have the support of the prime minister and the minister of national defence, even if they might have wavered on the issue. The challenge would be the great bureaucratic machine in Ottawa, which felt that this subject should have been discussed at length, with many options considered for a final approach. And so I apologized, begged forgiveness and got on with something else. If we had taken the Ottawa approach, some kind of decision would have been rendered months after the fact and would have been difficult to understand, much less implement. We still would have been forced to resolve the issue in the way we did, but meanwhile we would have lost the confidence of our troops that we would do what was right for them, and we would also have lost the confidence of Canadians in general. We would have achieved the opposite of the Vimy effect. What we did was right. Begging forgiveness cost me nothing, and the Canadian Forces came out of the small tempest with even more credibility.

CHAPTER 33

LEARN WITH YOUR TEAM

One of the great lessons we took from the men who had achieved the lightning victory over the Germans at Vimy Ridge in 1917—a Canadian victory that followed costly failures by the British and French, with horrible casualties—was how important it was to be a learning organization. If the organization was going to be a winning one, then the leaders, from the boss downward, also had to be that way. And if there if something that I remember about being the boss, it is that everybody pays attention to whatever the boss pays attention to. So if you as the boss believes it's important to continue to learn, pay attention to learning and so will everyone else.

The Canadian Forces had not been successful at continuing to learn. During the Cold War, each year was a repetition of the last, and the tactics, practised in training and not in war, had derived from the Second World War and had not changed since. Some leaders made small variations in exercises, but these changes lasted only as long as the individuals were in their jobs. None was captured in after-action reports, was turned into policy or drove training procedures, and they certainly never forced changes to the tactics, techniques and procedures that drove all our exercises and operations. We were using the same organizations, the same grouping of various skills and approaches that had been developed on the great British Army training establishment at Salisbury Plain in 1940–1944, and even though they sometimes later proved inappropriate in actual combat, they continued to shape our policies. We were determined to change that.

Most of the officers and soldiers who had been young and junior during the first post-Cold War operations in places like Somalia, Bosnia and Croatia were now senior leaders in the ranks of officers and senior non-commissioned officers. These officers were ready to ensure we did not repeat the mistakes of the past. Despite having not much of an idea of how to learn as an organization, we had put basic pieces in place, such as the Canadian Army Lessons Learned Centre. All the new system needed was some tender loving care. Former commanders like Mike Jeffery had put much focus on this change in our culture, and we were able to build on that.

The operation in southern Afghanistan, with our first battle casualties in the memory of most Canadians, brought with it a demand that we constantly improve, every day. At minimum, each contingent deploying for specific periods had to be better prepared than the one it was replacing, and that included improving how it deployed, how long it stayed, what it did and how it trained and prepared. Each area had to be adjusted as a result of the latest information, giving us knowledge that we could quickly put into action.

We started with our operational assessment cycle, made up of essentially four to six steps, beginning with observing (i.e., learning about the environment that marked the mission), orientating ourselves (taking steps to make us ready to achieve our mission, whether that was moving equipment, special training, deployments or intelligence actions), deciding on a plan of action and implementing it and then reassessing or learning from what had happened as a result. Then we started to prepare again. The reassessment step overlapped the observation step and the cycle was complete. To support the learning process in the army, we bolstered a lessons-learned capability in the air force and navy, while at the same time setting up a small team to help us learn what we could from our joint operations of air, land, sea and special forces.

Commanders like me had to insist on the after-action reviews, had to insist that the tough questions be asked, that those questions were followed up on and that those actions were compared against our present way of doing things to see what, if anything, needed to be changed. Lastly, we had to be forever alert that these changes were not put on the slow train and we that would not be waited out by those who were looking to protect past practices.

Although we were never perfect and often not even very good at this learning process, we had nonetheless started to change the culture. Learning started to become a way of life. I believed the Canadian Forces was like a ballistic missile. Our strategic vision was our far-off target; our land, sea, air and special force units were our warhead; the stages of our rocket were the people who generated those operational forces (the army, navy, air force and special forces command) and the folks in personnel command who took men and women from recruitment to retirement; and the force development team whose long-term ideas shaped our next generation of units and equipment were the tailfins that steered the missile on its way.

The operational lessons we had learned from missions overseas shaped those people carrying out the operations. The short-term lessons changed how the training and force generation commands were producing forces so that they could be successful. That is, they helped determine what tactics should be taught and what equipment used, as well as the mix of different skill sets each unit needed and what they had to be able to withstand on operations. The lessons reached further back to shape how we attracted and kept personnel, and shaped the future of the Canadian Forces.

Your organization or company becomes competitive and stays that way because the leaders know the environment and business better than their competitors. As the environment changes, however, and the company grows, if it is to not only survive but also thrive, a leader needs to learn small, tactical lessons and absorb the strategic implications.

One of the best chances to learn is from a poor leader. Sadly, these leaders, despite their negative qualities, are often ignored and the possibility of learning from them is lost. Don't dismiss bad leaders. Instead, watch what they do and learn from them. Learn what not to do. I learned two-thirds of everything I believe in about leadership from bad leaders. That included the boss who apologized for spending too much time in his office and not enough with the troops, the officer who held his troops to standards that he himself could not meet, drunks, autocrats and those who were insecure.

The story that for me brings to life the importance of learning is one about the Prussian king and general, Frederick the Great. The great campaigner owned a mule that he had taken on every one of his many campaigns, thirteen in all. Yet at the end of those thirteen campaigns, as the general noted to his staff one day, the mule was still a mule no matter how many experiences it had gone through.

My mantra became: Don't be a mule. The Canadian Forces certainly had become one during the 1990s. We spent some fifteen years in Bosnia, sending thousands of soldiers on six-month rotations that in the end really were thirty separate rotations. All because, like Frederick the Great's mule, we had refused to learn from past experiences, good or bad. So don't you be a mule. Learn yourself and make sure those in your company do as well. Drive the learning by paying personal attention to it, make it policy and then validate it in your training and, consequently, in the way you operate.

CHAPTER 34

PEEING ON THE ELECTRIC FENCE

Good judgment often comes as a result of bad experience, and bad experience is often the result of bad judgment. Poor judgment, in the right circumstances, can be a powerful learning tool that leads, in a forgiving organization with leaders who have acknowledged their own imperfections, to better knowledge and skills that may be applied in a vast number of situations. You *will* make mistakes. The key is to accept that this will occur and learn from those mistakes. Nobody is, or can be, perfect, so you as a leader must understand that about those you lead. For aspiring leaders, honest mistakes (not moral ones such as drunk driving or sexually harassing subordinates) are part of their mentoring or developmental process and shouldn't immediately lead to their termination.

The Texans at Fort Hood, where I used to live, say that you can learn about leadership by reading or watching others, but at the end of the day, sometimes you have to make the mistake—

peeing on the electric fence, if you will—all by yourself. I've peed on a lot of electric fences during my life and career, and have learned from every single, painful experience.

When the Canadian brigade was stationed in Germany, we moved our tank regiment, fifty-nine tanks, from one part of the country to another for training and operational readiness drills. One lucky officer was anointed as the train conducting officer, or TCO, with the responsibility for supervising the loading of tanks and other vehicles, and putting people in the bunker cars, and then overseeing the unloading at the destination.

I had observed other officers do this, gotten tips from them, read the TCO guidebook, quizzed my non-commissioned officers and learned as much as I thought I needed to know to do the job. I skipped the part, however, where detailed inspection of each tank's security on the railcar was verified and in particular did not see the need to check such things as the fastening of the tank gun barrels into the centre rear of the tank. One crew had been sloppy in its preparation and did not put in a simple cotter, or locking pin, when securing the gun barrel. During the trip, which took some twenty-four hours, the securing mechanism worked loose. Trying to explain to my squadron commander, the commanding officer of the regiment and to the Deutsche Bundesbahn authorities who ran the German train system why the gun barrel had swung freely during transit was not easy. Explaining why six miles of telephone poles (those situated on the outside of bends in the railway) had been destroyed was even more difficult. Lesson learned: Never miss the opportunity to verify the details and, if you can make time, check them twice. It's worth avoiding the pain.

I learned a lot from many people who became my mentors long before the term "mentors" became popular, and particularly from confident leaders who had already made the same mistakes I had. I survived those errors of judgment, and then was offered more challenges. I was much better prepared to meet the new challenges as a result. Don't let mistakes get you down or deter you from pursuing your goals.

KNOW WHEN TO SAY STOP

When you know when to say stop, you can restore confidence in yourself and your customers. When you don't know when to put the brakes on, it can cost you millions, drive away your customers and destroy the confidence people have in you. Sadly, I've seen many examples of when a leader should have said stop.

Many more than did should have yelled stop when the Canadian Forces and the Department of Defence were integrated back in the 1960s. The integration was completed at the same time as the army, navy and air force were unifying into the Canadian Forces. It was a step too far and was a major plank in the march to creating a bureaucracy out of the Forces, with men and women in uniform starting truly to think and behave like any other government department. One of those steps, the unification, was enough. The second, integration, was a bridge too far. Couple that with crummy uniforms, enormous cutbacks, and poor equipment and you have what was the first decade of darkness, which led to the second in the 1990s, and from which the Canadian Forces is only breaking out now. Unfortunately, momentum can quickly build up behind even the most obvious bad ideas, right from the time that they are first proposed and discussed.

The most valuable use of my time as a leader was to be around when stupid ideas were first raised, so that I had the opportunity to blow them to smithereens before they gained a life of their own. Occasionally, despite my best efforts, some did take flight. As well, what seemed like good ideas at the time were implemented but did not prove out. People had invested in those ideas and had spent a lot of money on them, but they needed to be stopped. Often the battle cry was that spending a few million dollars more, and putting more people on the job, would bring results. Reputations—in some cases entire careers—had been staked on the outcome. It is very difficult to stop a process in a big organization once this has taken place, even when it is evident to all concerned that change to the process is necessary. Sometimes we take leave of common sense, and even though we know that an idea will never fly, it takes us five years and millions of dollars to prove it.

Brigadier-General Pierre Lalonde, my former boss in army headquarters in Montreal, gave me great advice. When congratulating me for getting command of a regiment, he said, "Rick, I suppose you know what your most important job as a leader is."

"Of course," I replied. "I'm going to set the personal example, focus and then build a team that can accomplish the regiment's mission."

"Sure, that's important," said Pierre, "but the most important thing you do as a leader is to protect your soldiers from good ideas. No matter how good the idea, if you impose too many of them, you will kill your unit." It was good advice, but I also feel that as a leader you need not only to protect those you lead from too many good ideas but also to protect them from stupid ideas, and good ideas gone wrong. You need to have the courage to say no.

Here's an example that illustrates this need: the concept of leaderless branches at one of Canada's major banks. The concept was that within a specific branch, small, specialized groups would report to their own, unique chain of command. Someone had responsibility for the branch's infrastructure and reported to the person who had responsibility for infrastructure for a district or region. Others, those who opened customers' accounts, reported to a retail manager in charge of all the customer service representatives; those selling products reported to a superior who also had responsibility for sales teams in that district or region. What was not taken into account was that these branches were small and had an intimacy with their clientele, and that they operated in a very cohesive manner. Anything that went wrong in one part of the branch immediately affected another part. Quite quickly, their core business—attracting, satisfying and therefore keeping customers—was damaged by the new policy.

It was overwhelmingly obvious to those at the branches— that is, those who had to meet and work with their customers— that the concept didn't make much sense. Each branch needed to be a team, and that team needed one leader who could inspire them, represent them and take responsibility to make sure all parts were working together to serve customers and make the branch, the district, the region and the bank itself successful. Really, this idea should never have gotten off the ground because all those involved doing the job recognized that it would fail. But the bank executives in leadership positions could not say no. For several years they tried to make the concept work, enduring many disgruntled employees, unsatisfied customers and a precipitous drop in customer satisfaction. An idea that did not include the needs at the tactical level (branch) was doomed to failure but was changed only after years of customer anger.

Another example comes from the rush in the 1990s to become more efficient by using technology. The Department of National Defence wanted to establish a secure, closed computer network for its senior leaders to let them communicate, access sensitive files and work more effectively. Launched to the tune of several million dollars, the project rapidly became more important than its goal, and the focus became to develop a system that might even be sold to others. It was awkward to use, the increasing costs required to keep it running were enormous and it never quite succeeded in meeting the need for which the project had been started in the first place. The system quickly became a boondoggle. Careers, jobs and futures all became tied to the project for too many people, and it seemed nobody could say no. Finally, after years and millions of dollars wasted, it died a natural death when it became overwhelmingly obvious that people were not actually using the system. If someone had shut it down in the beginning, we could have saved those millions and allowed a greater focus on other, more important and realizable goals.

Another example is my trip to Kunduz, the provincial capital of the province of Kunduz, in northeast Afghanistan to visit the German provincial reconstruction team. I climbed on board a C-160 Transall transport plane and took my position at the back of the large cockpit, the two pilots just in front of me. The tower gave us clearance to taxi and take off. As the plane gathered speed heading down the runway, the pilots and I were shocked to see a Russian-built IL-76 transport plane on final approach and coming directly at us. Our pilot stood on the brakes and reversed the thrust, pulling hard to the right onto the last exit from the runway. The tail of our aircraft cleared the runway just before the IL-76 went through that space. Our plane stopped, and the crew swore at the tower, tearing a strip off the air traffic controller who'd cleared the plane to land while we were supposed to be taking off. As the pilots then joked, "We'll be ready to go after changing our underwear." We got ready to depart again with a now-chastened air traffic controller giving us priority.

In the second attempt to take off, we were about fifty metres in the air when something started going seriously wrong with the right engine. The C-160 is a two-engine aircraft and needs both to fly. The engine was smoking and leaving bits and pieces behind. It seemed obvious that a foreign object had been sucked into the engine's air intakes. The crew, professional in the extreme, declared an emergency. They made a 180-degree turn and landed safely. We all scrambled off the aircraft and, once clear, the command pilot said he'd have another aircraft for me in about forty minutes. "Stand down," I said. "I think I have tested my luck enough. I'm not going to Kunduz today." I've never felt that I made the wrong decision in that instance. Saying "stop" probably reflected my belief that our luck, at least for that day, was used up.

Having the ability, and at times the courage, to say no is a critical part of being a leader. Although much of a leader's business is going forward, sometimes the fastest method to get ahead is to put an end to something that just isn't working, is detracting from a focus on the mission and is actually bringing you back compared to your competitors.

CHAPTER 36

STAND ON YOUR SOAPBOX

I have always believed that power is useless unless you exercise it. As a leader, you will likely be given certain opportunities by dint of your appointment, and you are undercutting yourself, and those you lead, if you don't take advantage and use them. For one, it's important to take advantage of your soapbox, that is, the platform on which you can articulate your direction, the challenges you are facing and what you need to overcome those challenges, and to be able to do it in a manner that gets attention and action.

For the longest time, this was something that I had not really thought about, although after reading Lewis MacKenzie's book *The Road to Sarajevo* it should have been obvious to me. As commander of the UN mission in Sarajevo, Lew said that his most powerful weapon was publicity, showing people around the world the tragedy unfolding in the Balkans, complete with riveting pictures. Lew was plagued by indecisiveness at UN Headquarters in New York but quickly learned that even a group as slow to act as the UN Security Council could be forced to make the occasional decision and take action when the situation was on television screens and across front pages around the world.

We had already gained some experience in the power of the press to rivet Canadians during the Red River Flood and ice storm operations, and saw more good examples during the Kosovo air war, when Walt Natynczyk was the face and voice letting Canadians know what was happening. We had the ability to get the nation's attention. The media became the vehicle to address Canadians frankly about their military and to bring them onside with our efforts, and it was just that, a vehicle. I did not, for example, talk to the journalists so much as speak directly through the TV or still camera to up to 35 million citizens. It was direct communication at its best.

Our best ambassadors, from my perspective, have always been our front-line troops, and that's who we wanted on the soapbox. We shared footage of our troops during a Remembrance Day ceremony and set up an interview with some of those who had just completed a heroic deed. We also allowed the filming of a soldier going about her business while being shot at in Kandahar; of young sailors on the deck of a Canadian frigate in the Horn of Africa region, with responsibility for security of the immense amount of shipping passing through there each day; and of our Snowbirds, the best aerobatic pilots and aircraft maintainers in the world. Each on his or her own was a winner; in combination they made Canadians fiercely proud of whom they were, what they did and how well they represented them. Each was truly one of Canada's sons or daughters.

We didn't waste much time on comprehensive communication strategies that became outdated before we'd finished writing them. With the assistance of Tom Ring, our assistant deputy minister for communications, and intelligent public affairs officers such Rita LePage, Holly Apostoliuk and Cindy Tessier, we pretty much had our messages down, based on the meat of our actions. During that time, I continued with my approach of always telling the truth, no matter how unwelcome it was. This meant too that I did not have to try to keep my story straight. As my dad used to say, "If you don't lie, you don't have to remember anything." A lot of wisdom there.

Lastly, we built on initial success. Riding the wave of support for the troops led us to reinforce just what it was they were doing so well for us and led to more support for them and their families. The soapbox is not just the vehicle for the voice, it *is* the voice of the commander or senior leader standing on the box. Not everyone was happy with my message, but the dissent actually raised my soapbox higher and it helped me to change the culture of the Canadian Forces.

Determine what kind of soapbox you have, how big it is, if it affects internal or external possibilities or both and use it to maximum effect. Remember, messages are meaningless unless the meat is visible through your actions. Launch and expect criticism, but continually reassess and carry on. After all, did you take your appointment to preside over a status quo or to actually make some change? If it's the latter, build that soapbox!

PART 5

GETTING IT RIGHT

CREDIBILITY IS YOUR CENTRE OF GRAVITY

Honest people expect to be believed. They have strong influence and can have a powerful impact merely because of the moral way they behave. They know that others believe them by default. Similarly, great leaders hold to the steadfast belief that their credibility is crucial to their ability to lead. Building trust is at the centre of their every thought and action, and directly enables them to achieve their goals. Without credibility, they simply are not effective.

When you have credibility, people trust that you and your team are trying to achieve honourable goals. They also trust that your decisions are made with the greater good in mind, and not simply because of what's best for your career, for your wallet or for any other selfish reason. Leaders who have credibility can achieve great things simply because of it. Mahatma Gandhi's integrity and resulting credibility gave him the strength to change the world. Conversely, executives at financial institutions who blatantly lie, police officers who collaborate with other police officers to change their stories and politicians who are on the take are clearly examples of people without credibility and of those who can never be effective as leaders. Sadly, they also detract from the credibility of the rest of the leaders in their organizations and, overall, from the organization itself.

That credibility can achieve great things may sound like lofty words, a pie-in-the-sky discussion, but really, it's only practical. As a soldier, every action I took and every word I spoke was taken and spoken with a view to first building my credibility as a person and as a leader. I knew that the sailors, soldiers, airmen and airwomen would work wonders to change the Canadian Forces with me if they saw me as their leader, someone they would be proud, not embarrassed, to follow. If they hadn't, we never would have effected real change. I knew, too, that if the civilians who supported those of us in uniform saw me as credible in the role of Chief of the Defence Staff, they too, even in the difficult environment of minority government Ottawa, would fully support us in achieving all that we sought. My role as a leader was important for disparate other groups, such as military families, elected officials, Canadians in general and even our allies. Credibility does not come easily or without work and courage.

In difficult times, people are unsettled and look for vision from their leaders to settle them down. If they believe what you're saying, they will weather any storm with much less stress than they would otherwise because of the confidence they have in you. They trust you will do the right thing, and their confidence in you is highly contagious.

Lack of credibility, however, leads to a lack of confidence. If other leaders in the company don't trust your truthfulness, commitment and loyalty, you will never be able to inspire your troops.

We had to build others' confidence in the Canadian Forces. In the eyes of the troops, there was a void in the domain of visible leadership. The military needed someone who spoke plainly, was absolutely honest in everything he or she did and had the courage to do what was necessary, not just to talk a good game. The Canadian Forces didn't need someone who was politically correct or who held a partisan political view. Quite simply, the troops wanted to feel proud of serving Canada in our nation's uniform. The vast majority had lost much of that pride during the 1990s. Military families, under enormous stress as well, also wanted to know their place in our country. Everyday Canadians wanted to know why they should invest their scarce dollars in us, and the Liberals and Conservatives wanted to see themselves reflected in us and what we were doing so that they could get re-elected after investing millions, even billions, in rebuilding the Canadian Forces.

So, to borrow a friend's phrase, I spoke truth to power by simply telling the truth and trying my best to not colour the situation in any "Ottawa" way. I said what I believed, and if that changed over time and because of circumstances, I said that too. From day one, following the change of command parade, with my actions and words I tried to fill the leadership void.

My frank approach caused more than a few politicians to sputter and led to some backstabbing in the corridors of power that put pressure on me and sometimes my family. For example, the Prime Minister's Office (PMO) made a mistake when it said, without consulting the Canadian Forces, that we'd have the Kandahar mission completed by 2011. There was no way I was going to let something like that stand. Our credibility, and mine, was at stake. The PMO forgot that journalists, soldiers and many Canadians had a pretty good idea of the challenges and what was happening on the ground. It was sheer politicking, and I wanted no part of it.

I happened to be in Kandahar at the time, and after the announcement I was ambushed by several journalists, all of whom knew the PMO's line to be a lot of malarkey. So did every one of our soldiers and most Canadians. I told the reporters that it was going to take us ten years or more to build the kind of institutions needed to maintain an army, from staff colleges that produce competent senior commanders to logistics teams that can maintain the increasingly complex and modern equipment being delivered. We can leave in 2011 if our government decides that is what we must do, but make no mistake: the job will not be finished and someone else will have to do it.

As I've said, there was no way I could let the PMO's statement stand. Avoiding the issue would have created a perception of cowardice, since the practical assessment of things happening on the ground was obvious to all. The PMO's response to my words was to say that *it* knew the mission and could make the proper assessment, an answer that lacked all credibility and was simply ridiculous.

Establish credibility in everything you do, work hard to maintain it and avoid the slippery slope of following the party line. You will have to work hard all your life to build your credibility, but one slip-up can destroy it completely, so be constantly aware of the dangers to you and your reputation. With credibility you can begin to change the world. Without it, your most overwhelming job will be to change yourself, leaving little time or energy to accomplish much else.

PERCEPTION IS REALITY

A BBC reporter came to Germany in 2004 to address the soldiers who would be part of my International Security Assistance Force (ISAF) staff. As part of the preparatory period for our taking command of the ISAF mission in Afghanistan, the roughly two hundred men and women from some thirty-five-plus countries received instruction in many subjects, including the media and communication, and how to use both in pursuit of our goals. "You may think yourselves the most capable force in the world, and that may be true," the reporter said, "but if the perception is that you are losing the battle, that will become the reality. The perception—that you are losing—will bolster your enemy's courage and tenacity, causing him to take more risks, attack you more frequently and strike in places where he should be fearful of treading. It will also weaken your allies—their commitment to staying with the mission and the resolve of troop-contributing countries to provide the necessary people, resources and flexibility to complete the job will wane and thus deny you the ability to shape the future." His profound words had a lasting impact on me as we embarked on fundamental change for the Canadian Forces, and what he said is particularly apt at this dangerous stage of the Afghan mission.

Our own men and women, both military and civilian, had to believe that what we were setting out to achieve was going to be not just radical but also essential, that radical changes were driven by overwhelming need and that these changes would continue after I left. In short, we'd stop only when the vision was fully implemented. Our government, no matter which party held the reins of power, had to see value, in terms of potential votes, in what we were doing. I really wanted to believe that our governing party would see value in enhancing Canada's stature and influence around the world, and helping guarantee our stability and security at home. However, I spent a lot of time around Ottawa and, sadly, I hold the parties that form our governments in contempt. Their first and only concern is staying in power. They will do anything to achieve that. Only if we could help a party stay in office were we of value to it. Truly, it was important how the Liberals and Conservatives perceived us, our value and the value of what we were doing. The Bloc and NDP were inconsequential.

Most important, Canadians across this great land had to believe that we would be relevant to them and worthy of the investment needed to realize our vision. Many Canadians still believed that the Canadian Forces should be ashamed to show its face in public (my wife was told that one day), and the anti-military attitudes that had developed in Canada over three or four decades were still prevalent in many parts of Ottawa and our society in general. We had our work cut out for us.

People form their perceptions based on the smallest, often most trivial, events. Often they are based on one-off incidents. The Royal Canadian Mounted Police provides a good example of this. For more than one hundred years, the RCMP, now over twenty thousand strong, have been icons in our country, with a reputation of being among the very best—in my view, *the* best— of the world's police forces. Yet the RCMP's reputation has been dramatically damaged by a few isolated incidents, the best known of which was the death of a Polish man at the Vancouver airport. The bad judgment of a few, and the belief by many Canadians that those few, the individual police officers involved, had coordinated afterwards to protect themselves, changed dramatically how Canadians view the RCMP generally, no matter how great the force really is. Nothing has occurred in Ottawa to change that view. One can only imagine how it affects the work and life of every single man and woman wearing the Red Serge, each region and the force itself. This loss of confidence means that every one of the RCMP's actions is judged more harshly, and its actions are often pilloried for what would normally be worthy of kudos. Perception has become a harsh reality for the RCMP.

The Canadian Forces had its work cut out to dissociate itself from a widely held opinion that we were merely civil servants in another kind of suit, and a waste of money to boot. That perception infuriated the troops. Realistically, many Canadians no longer saw our men and women in uniform as soldiers but as peacekeepers. The troops were infuriated by this also, believing rightly that they were one of the few armed forces in the world that could do the spectrum of operations, from peacekeeping to war fighting, and that that was the defining description of a modern soldier. When, in the late 1990s, several media releases dealing with the NATO mission in Bosnia referred to the deployment of British, Dutch, American and Canadian peacekeepers, the air around those already deployed in Bosnia turned blue as they, proud soldiers, vented their frustrations.

We had to change this perception because it prevented us from doing all the things we, and the Government of Canada, believed we needed to do on behalf of our country. We needed the "shine" on us to attract kids to join, because without them we would fail. We needed the investment to renew our equipment fleets, to conduct training and to build teams, develop leaders and maintain readiness. After all, we were soldiers, sailors, airmen and airwomen, as capable in our profession as any in the world and capable of doing much more on behalf of our country than credited. Our message resonated with ordinary Canadians—the Tim Hortons crowd—and gradually, the rest of the country took notice. But it took a lot of work, and although I took some heck for publicly saying we were the Canadian Forces and not just another government department, and that our job was to be able to kill people, it certainly was the start of Canadians paying attention to what their sons and daughters in uniform were capable of doing.

Some things could not be changed. We in the Canadian Forces had challenges similar to those the RCMP faced, the most memorable being the enduring, negative legacy of the Somalian mission. Many saw the Somalia mission in the 1990s as a disaster, and therefore it became one. Thousands of men and women in uniform believe that, overall, Somalia was a successful mission. They were proud of what they and others did, believed in their

264

work and were as frustrated as any Canadian by the actions of a few, who quickly became the face of many. Our soldiers, with those one or two widely publicized exceptions, did an awesome job. Trying to defend that mission, however, became a waste of energy, and our strategy was to not try. We simply said that we had learned and changed and were the armed forces Canadians wanted. The lesson is, don't defend what cannot be defended; simply move forward.

Changing the perception that we were a waste of money was easier than anything else. Obviously, the mission in Afghanistan helped, with the commitment of our people and their dedication so heartwarmingly obvious through the eyes of the embedded journalist program. Their need for equipment particularly, to do the dangerous work they had to do, was clear. Equally powerful to external missions, however, was simply pointing out to audiences across the country, using every venue and vehicle possible, that more than ten thousand of these men and women were on duty in Canada each and every day, helping to provide security for the great life and society we have. A few examples—fighter pilots interdicting Russian Bears (long-range bombers) that flew close to our airspace in the North; search and rescue technicians who routinely and with great courage saved the lives of unfortunate, and sometimes stupid, Canadians whose lives were at risk, among others—convinced even the most stubborn that what we did was relevant to them and was worthy of investment. After all, a fighter pilot without a plane could intercept no aircraft, however skilled he or she is.

Thousands of Canadians have come up to me in these last few years saying, "General, we love the work you're doing in the Canadian Forces and the changes you're making, and we want you to know we support you." They would tell me they spoke to their Members of Parliament about us, had thanked uniformed individuals, supported military families and grieved with survivors. If I had asked any one of them what changes they liked in particular, and what had changed their minds about the Canadian Forces, not one of them would have been able to give me an answer. They did not have the facts to understand exactly what we were doing, but the public perception of the Forces and the changes it was undergoing was extremely positive and a combat multiplier for all that we were trying to achieve. Clearly, the perception had shifted positively in our direction.

It is no different in your organization. Creating the positive perception takes vision, good people, skilful communicators, solid messages based on values and actions and lots of good luck. Once created, the positive perception is truly a multiplier of your efforts and must be safe-guarded at all costs. Negative perceptions are often impossible to change. The difference between the two can mean success or failure, so there's no point arguing that what your customers believe is not the reality. If they believe it, it is reality, and you will have to change what you are to change how they view you.

TAKE THE ROCKS OUT OF THE RUCKSACK

When soldiers pack their rucksacks, they quickly learn there is a tipping point. Each item, as it goes into the rucksack, seems like a valuable asset: can't go without socks, knife, camera, ammo, sleeping bag, and so on. Even soldiers can forget that all of these items add up and if too much is loaded in and the rucksacks are too heavy on their backs, they will topple over. And no soldier, however good, can accomplish much lying on his or her back.

As a leader, you need to ensure that you don't overfill the rucksacks of those in your command and cause them to topple over. In fact, your job as a leader is to take the rocks (those things that detract from doing the job) out of the rucksacks of those you lead, making them more agile, flexible and competitive, and therefore capable of being overwhelmingly successful in helping achieve your mission.

I have had the privilege to witness incredible courage in

my life as a soldier, whether it was seeing young men or women do high-risk jobs because that was what their professions called for or watching people step up when others were fearful. Putting your life on the line is part of being a soldier. Physical courage has never been in short supply in Canadian servicemen and -women. The torch, handed to this generation from our forefathers on Vimy Ridge, in Normandy, on the North Atlantic, in the skies over Britain and from the frozen hills of Korea has been held high indeed. During Operation Medusa in Afghanistan, for example, when the Canadian contingent broke the Taliban offensive to take Kandahar City, I saw incredible examples of individual acts of valour, some of which have been recognized by the Governor General on behalf of our country.

Take Master Corporal Collin Fitzgerald, who was awarded a Medal of Military Valour. In the words of his accompanying letter of commendation, he was recognized for

> his selfless and valiant actions carried out on 24 May 2006 during an ongoing enemy ambush under intense, accurate enemy fire. Master Corporal Fitzgerald repeatedly exposed himself to enemy fire by entering and re-entering a burning platoon vehicle and successfully driving it off the roadway, permitting the remaining vehicles trapped in the enemy zone to break free.

His courageous and completely selfless actions were instrumental to his platoon's successful operation and to getting that platoon out of a kill zone that the enemy had smartly laid out. They helped save the lives of his fellow platoon members, who were caught out by a much larger Taliban force, without readily available reinforcements, in very difficult country.

Collin, who now lives in Morrisburg, Ontario, was in a bar with a friend one night after returning home when he was surrounded by a group and attacked. He was beaten severely with fists and a bottle and kicked mercilessly while being taunted with, "What kind of hero are you now?" Sadly, an attack like this, by those who live the great lives they do in part because of the heroism and valour of Collin and his battle buddies, demeans us all. Collin deserved better.

Private Jess Larochelle was manning an observation post in Pashmul, Afghanistan, when it was destroyed by an enemy rocket. Although he was alone, severely injured and under sustained enemy fire in his exposed position, he aggressively provided covering fire over the otherwise undefended flank of his company's position. Although two personnel, Sergeant Darcy Tedford and Private Blake Williamson, were killed and three others were wounded in the initial attack, Jess's heroic actions permitted the remainder of the company to defend their position and successfully fend off the sustained attack of more than twenty insurgents. His valiant conduct saved the lives of many members of his company. Jess is one of those quiet young men who *do* things as opposed to just talking about doing things.

When people who work for you demonstrate such incredible courage—not just the physical courage like that shown by Collin and Jess but also moral courage, such as when they have the courage to hold you accountable for what you will deliver as their leader, for how will you perform as their leader in representing them on your battlefield—it needs to be recognized.

In short, they will judge you, in part, based on the success you have had taking those rocks out of their rucksacks so they can do what you have asked of them and have the maximum chance of surviving the experience.

My battlefields as Chief of the Defence Staff were at NATO, headquartered in Brussels and Ottawa. As a junior officer, I had worked under numerous brutally ineffective ministers of national defence, who had only a negative affect as a result of their bully behaviour within the department and their pussycat behaviour outside it, allowing the Department of National Defence and the Canadian Forces to be punched from pillar to post. I was determined to fight the battles for those who defined courage for me on a daily basis—to take rocks out of their rucksacks—and I was determined to be equal to their efforts. It was not always easy, and it didn't happen instantly.

No issue in Ottawa or NATO was ever clear-cut and hence the rocks were different and sometimes difficult to recognize. This kind of bureaucracy and the way it works has been described as the "death of a thousand cuts," which I have found holds true for most private companies and institutions also. Things happen, one at a time, with almost imperceptible movement, and each small step is so insignificant in and of itself that it usually affords no opportunity to draw a line in the sand and say stop. A clear example of this was the case for continued expansion of NATO in Afghanistan, either to help with security for the elections or to take responsibility for the international mission throughout. The mission had clearly stated requirements: attack and transport helicopters, unmanned aerial vehicles (UAVs), fixed-wing aircraft, battalions of troops, reconstruction units in the form of provincial reconstruction teams, headquarters, special forces, and so on. Only when these were provided would NATO assist in the election security, expand its area of operations or, in fact, do what it had said it would do. What then happened was predictable. Some of the helicopters would be provided, but not quite the number needed (which was invariably the absolute minimum assessed to be necessary), some of those promised would not be available for months and the mixture of attack versus transport helicopters would be different from that needed. The UAVs would show, often concentrated in one spot and just as often dedicated to national, as opposed to alliance, use. The transport aircraft were always in shorter supply than demand and were restricted as to what and where they would fly. Most important, countries were never eager to commit more ground troops, so they always fell dramatically short of requirements. Since these challenges came up individually, it became very difficult to say no to changes, restrictions or impediments. None of us, though, was in any doubt that we were throwing rocks in the rucksacks of those actually executing the mission. Overwhelming conditions for success had not been set, yet the momentum for continued expansion of NATO in Afghanistan became impossible to stop.

The problem was compounded by the restrictions many nations put on what they had finally provided: where their troops could be deployed and what they were allowed to do, for example. A nation's government would offer troops to NATO but then dictate which part of Afghanistan they were allowed to go—or more often, which parts they were *not* allowed to go to, which meant the NATO commander had no flexibility to put forces where they were most needed to win the fight. That fight was very dangerous in some areas and benign in others. Thus, although the totals of troops available might finally seem impressive, only a minority were available where they were needed. These were heavy rocks indeed, and the tipping point was always in question.

The thousand cuts in Brussels started out being more obvious. The military commanders always started with a clear message: This is what we need and we will not recommend doing it with less. Pressure from national capitals mounted unrelentingly during NATO meetings. Invariably, it would have an impact: "Well, we have four helos and we need ten; we've been promised two more, one for certain, and we think we should be able to do the job with eight. If we really need them, two more are on alert in Europe to deploy." The same occurred with the rest of the requirements. Even if you could get along with four helicopters, you would have only about 50 percent of the required troops and, out of that 50 percent, fully 40 percent were in benign areas where there was no risk.

I used the rocks in the rucksack analogy for us Canadians also to describe the impact of actions on Canadian commitments and deployments. "Look," I said, "we are putting a commander in charge of this mission, with responsibility to execute it successfully and accountability to us to do so, but with little to no authority in how he or she can do it. It's as if we put a rucksack on his back, and every time he turns around, we throw in another rock. Sorry, you cannot have all the troops you need because the government has said you can only have a thousand and they won't change position on that. No, you cannot have everyone you need for pre-deployment training, they have jobs to do right up until they leave and, no, you cannot make those decisions, they must be made in Ottawa, and so on. Eventually, we should not be surprised when the weight of rocks in the rucksack on the commander's back causes him to fall on his ass."

My job as a leader was to match the peerless physical courage described earlier with moral courage at NATO and in Ottawa, and to lift the rocks out of the rucksack. I don't mind admitting that I was often clumsy, but I was always direct in what I said. I was driven every day to set conditions for the commander and the team to succeed. After visiting any of our missions, in Canada or abroad, I always recommitted to doing my part to get things done, as opposed to talking about getting things done. My moral courage had to be equal to the courage of Jess Larochelle and Collin Fitzgerald, as well as to the fortitude shown by Mike Denine, Pat Tower and all the rest who made us so proud on those terrible days of fighting and dying. I fought hard to take the rocks out of the rucksack. If we were going to ask men and women to do dangerous jobs, we had to equip them for it. I said, "Don't tell me that you can't, because if you can't, then you should admit you are asking those sons and daughters serving our country to carry a disproportionate burden on their shoulders because the other 35 million Canadians won't carry their share."

This moral stand wasn't easy. Sometimes it was not clear when, or even if, I should take a stand because each one of the thousand cuts was in itself so benign. When I did take a stand, there were a thousand people with a thousand reasons trying to change my decision. I reaffirmed my commitment and responsibility to our men and women and, through them, to Canada, every day. In my mind, I worked to lead from the front, to look after our troops and to learn every day how to proceed in a better way.

It is no different for you as a leader. Take the rocks out of the rucksacks of those you lead. Lighten their loads, make them more agile, quicker to respond, more competitive and, ultimately, more successful. Keep a tin can on your desk and every time you feel that something detrimental is being done to detract from achieving your goals, throw a rock into the can. Then take action until you feel enough has been done to take the rock back out. Keep the tipping point on the positive side in everything you do.

FIRST REPORTS ARE ALWAYS WRONG

One of the things I learned early on during operations, especially during stressful times, was that first reports are always wrong, second reports are always almost entirely wrong and third reports are usually wrong. When it's dark and people are tired and afraid, crises get exaggerated. Somehow, a group of twenty enemy soldiers become two hundred, or two thousand. I once read a comment from a soldier on the front lines of the Korean War, who was rightly cynical about the media hysteria over the Chinese "human wave" attacks. "Yes," he told a reporter, "we were attacked by a human wave last night, and I shot him." Regardless of training, until people get practical experience in what they are doing, you must view with a jaundiced eye initial reports stating that they've achieved world domination or that the sky has fallen.

This means taking care in how you react in a developing crisis. Yes, take prudent preparatory measures, but get the "ground truth" before you take any big steps. If you fail to do so, you may take unwarranted, wasteful, even terribly harmful actions. Things are never as good or as bad as they first seem, so don't overreact. Training, learning and more training can improve the first reactions but only when you combine them with experience do things get much better. You'll never make your initial responses perfect, and rarely will you even make them good, but you can improve them.

I was the victim of first reports many times in my life, but one incident, when I was ISAF (International Security Assistance Force) commander in Kabul, Afghanistan, in 2004, stands out. Afghanistan had known thirty years of extended violence and destruction, with rotating governments, and the stabilization process was just under way. One of our constant concerns was the survival of the government, including the survival of the Afghanistan president, Hamid Karzai, himself. We were helping to bring the so-called warlords into the political process and, at the same time, trying to persuade them to give up their militia forces, tanks, artillery and other spoils of war and tools of power. There was enormous pressure on those militia forces to do all of that, tensions were high and the approaching election would cement many of the new power arrangements. We constantly worried about a coup, an assassination and a return to the civil war of the past that would destroy all that had been built so far.

These concerns all came to a head in the early hours of 1 April 2004. I was awakened by one of the duty officers and asked to come to the operations centre at our headquarters, immediately across from the US Embassy in Kabul. When I arrived, it was obvious that something unusual was going on. All of the desks, normally empty during these mostly quiet hours, were occupied by busy staff officers. I was soon brought up to speed: there had been a shooting near the presidential palace in Kabul.

Rockets were routinely fired into Kabul from the surrounding hills, and suicide bombers had struck inside the city several times, but those were distant attacks or, more accurately, attacks from a distance. This direct assault, if that indeed was what we were seeing, was a much more ominous indicator of more serious things to come. We progressed quickly through a variety of elements in the operational plans we had developed for just such a contingency. An unmanned aerial vehicle (UAV) was readied and then launched from the German brigade to give us real-time visuals from the scene without being intrusive or inflaming the situation. The signals intelligence units were put to work, and liaison officers were hustled out the door to quiz our many contacts, foreign and Afghan, throughout the city. Our Quick Reaction Force, from the Norwegian and British contingents, was readied for action and started its movement to previously selected sites close to the palace. Our superior headquarters in Europe, the NATO Headquarters at Brunssum, the Netherlands, was notified, because if this was indeed an assassination attempt—as the first reports led us to suspect—diplomatic pressure on the warlords responsible would be one of our most powerful tools, and European diplomats would have to help coordinate that pressure. We reviewed the emergency extraction plans for the president; readied the next logical set of forces for whatever might be happening; ensured our brothers in arms in the US command, under my friend Lieutenant-General Dave Barno, were aware; and awaited the next reports, from all sources. The operations centre was a beehive of activity, and the energy increased even more when the next report came in.

"There is shooting," said the report, "between Afghan National Army soldiers and Kabul City Police officers."

This indicated a potential coup or assassination attempt by one, with opposition from the other. In any case, shooting between the two groups representing all that was new about Afghanistan and its hope for the future was serious indeed. It was still the middle of the night, and although they seemed to take ages to arrive, the reports and activities followed one after the other only minutes apart. More forces were being activated now, and the Kabul Multinational Brigade (under a German commander who worked for me) was getting a warning order to seal the downtown and assume control of all routes leading to and from the presidential palace, even at the risk of irritating one or another of our new Afghan partners. We didn't know where the threat was coming from, whether it was from one part of Kabul or another or even from outside the capital, and we had to be sure of anyone we let near the president.

The third, and fortunately final, report arrived soon after the second. "There has been," it said, "a *shouting*, between Afghan National Army soldiers and Kabul City Police near the presidential palace."

In reality, we had been on high alert because of a typo! The relief that flowed through the operations centre was palpable. I laughed so hard I almost cried. Our forces were stood down, the UAV landed and we all went back to bed, with our worst nightmares unrealized.

My point is simple: Understand the situation and don't get caught unawares, but realize that things will probably never be as good or bad as you have been led to believe they are. You have to trust your direct reports, and your sources of information and knowledge must be comprehensive, but you still must regard with skepticism any statement that makes it sound as if the sky is falling or Christ has returned. Acting too quickly will destroy your credibility and effectiveness just as thoroughly as acting too slowly and failing to meet the need.

CHAPTER 41

THE TIME IS ALWAYS RIGHT TO DO WHAT'S RIGHT

As I wrote at the beginning of this book, all of my points on leadership connect; none stands alone, and all relate back to people. The one I make in this chapter is no different. Far too many times in my life I've met people who had, in their own words, stored up their best ideas for when they would get the chance to be the boss. In other words, they had put brainstorming on hold, bottled their innovative ideas and gone along with the status quo so as to not disrupt their career paths, all with the intent of implementing change when they got to the top.

Those folks disturbed me, though I knew that few of them, perhaps none, would ever get to the top. These people are like a bottle filled with good air, sealed and left on a shelf for twenty years. One day, yearning for fresh, unpolluted air, you open the bottle, only to discover it has disappeared and all that's left is the bad air that's already all around you.

And so it is with people who sit on their hands until they become the boss. Their ideas become stale, and they have not shaped those ideas or earned credibility by implementing them through their actions. Their logic has not been poked at and twisted, truly challenged, by others. These individuals are bankrupt. To me, the time is always right to do what is right. I might have had ideas that would also work well down the road, but unless I tried them, I really wouldn't know whether they worked. And when there is pressure not to do something, it is often because of many of the reasons I discussed earlier—risk aversion, political correctness or partisanship. Waiting for conditions to be perfect to implement an idea means you will never do it.

Don't wait: the time to make change, to inspire others with new ideas, is always now.

CHAPTER 42

GO WITH YOUR GUT

Waiting to launch a plan or a project until you have everything so complete and detailed that it would be the marvel of MBA seminars at Harvard is hardly ever possible, at least not in the real world. The trick is being able to determine when the right time is to launch, react, respond or do nothing. You have to assess the environment, prepare to do what you need to do, start doing it, readjust based on what you see happening (and what your competition is doing) and do all of it faster and more efficiently than anyone else. If you do that, your team and your company will win out.

Metrics or measurements are the mainstay of many businesses. I have always been mistrustful of putting too much faith in metrics because I have become cynical about measuring things, particularly the things that really count. What I have found is that most of the time we measure what we can, not necessarily what's important, and that we spend a lot of time, energy and resources doing so. Most of the important stuff is about people, who are notoriously unpredictable, and so measuring people is a subjective business.

In Bosnia, I watched one of the two other divisions besides ours that was conducting operations there put enormous effort into capturing and measuring their activities: the number of miles their troops had driven, the area they had covered, the number of days their people were out on patrol, the number of patrols, the number of people out on patrol and on and on. It seemed to me that about 50 percent of the combat unit's effort was spent on measuring what the other 50 percent of effort was. In my opinion, it still didn't tell them anything that could help better shape progress toward the implementation of the Dayton Peace Accords and a better life for the three ethnic groups making up the country. For starters, their trying to define exactly what a patrol was puzzled me. Was a patrol something like ten vehicles with thirty soldiers driving through an area at speed, isolated from the populace they were trying to help? Or was it three soldiers on foot, moving slowly, weapons in a non-threatening position, and stopping to talk with locals at every possible chance, determining attitudes, needs and morale?

In Afghanistan, the metric was sorties flown, rounds fired, patrols conducted, training numbers of Afghan police, and number of days they were trained. Nothing was measured that actually helped a commander make decisions at any level to make progress implementing the mission. To the police, it didn't matter how many had been trained, for how long or how much equipment they had been given. All you had to do was speak to the local people and after fifteen seconds you would know whether they trusted the police or not. It was that simple. This unfortunately flies in the face of popular theory on reducing risk, but the reality is that people will make you succeed or fail and those people cannot be measured with objective metrics.

Learn to trust your gut. My gut instinct was shaped by every event I had ever been involved with. The same can be said of yours, and it knows more about people than any metric in existence. If you are visible in your organization, spend time with those you lead and develop strong relationships with those important to you, you will have the important measurements already and can, relying on that "gut" feeling, be able to make the right, big decisions. Don't become fearful of doing so. At every opportunity, challenge experts in what is measured and how it is measured and what it tells you. You, the leader, will often know the business better than anyone else, so use your gut to give you the competitive edge.

PART 6

TAKE CARE OF YOURSELF

COMMAND IS LONELY

President Truman's famous sign on his desk that read "The Buck Stops Here" was a very real indicator of the weight and responsibility resting on his shoulders. This kind of great responsibility, with the resultant stress, often leads to isolation from others. Some handle it well, others not so much. Isolation can be dangerous: it can cause increased paranoia and a decreased ability to think through ideas with others and have them challenge your thought process, which limits your effectiveness.

What perhaps was most difficult for me was that I was constantly "on show," as many leaders are. From the time I stepped out my door to the time I returned home, I had to be watchful of what I said and did, because somebody, somewhere, was watching, listening to or photographing me. Actions speak loudly, and for leaders, this is true of even the most minor of actions, particularly when it concerns people. Caught up in a whirlwind schedule, on the run almost all the time, it was, unfortunately, easy to give people the impression I was brushing them off. I really had to work at slowing things down, to ensure I had enough time with people and to avoid cramming too much into any one visit.

When I was at Fort Hood, Texas, the signals brigade commander, Colonel Carroll Pollett (now a lieutenant-general), organized the first of many visits for me to his brigade to see its capabilities and meet as many of his soldiers as possible. We had scheduled separate visits to two battalions, plus routine briefings, in a period of about three hours. I blew through the time allocated to meeting the first group of solders, those who provided satellite communications directly to commanders wherever they were. These incredibly capable young men and women almost always laboured in obscurity, never seen unless something went wrong. They reminded me of flowers in a desert: pour even the smallest amount of water, or in this case attention, on them and they blossomed.

I paid attention, all right—we spent the first three hours of our limited time with the first fifty people we met. I said to Carroll, "I cannot just be another drive-by visitor or general. They do great work for us and deserve recognition and appreciation. This visit is my way of showing both." My point is that if you don't pay attention to those who want to be led by you because you are disorganized—if you allow others to cram too many things into your schedule or you have not ensured flexibility to make sure you can do what's right—you need to change. Those you lead will observe you on the run all the time, and you may inadvertently blow them off. If you do, they will withdraw, and your command will be even lonelier than before.

I discovered too that many people wanted to use me for their own ends. This caused me to deliberately withdraw from some of them and to ask myself what they wanted, and to be ruthless when figuring out the answer. Interestingly, far too many did not care how tired, frazzled, depressed or broken I was on any given day, as long as they got their fifteen minutes of value from me. It would have been relatively easy to become cynical about people, but I quickly focused on my true friends and then met so many more positive and powerfully inspiring people that I always remained inspired.

You need to find balance, and investing in your family will go a long way toward that. Despite the intense demands of my job as Chief of the Defence Staff, my family, which had made its own sacrifices, became my refuge. My wife, Joyce, sons Chris and Steven, daughter-in-law Caroline and future daughter-in-law Amanda and, especially, grandsons Jack and Matthew helped me keep life on an even keel in my last years in uniform. Jack didn't care that I was a general or a leader. I was simply his Poppy, and that brought me down to earth easily. Matthew thought that a general served to lift him high up in my arms so he could be face to face with others.

Establishing a supportive team of personal staff, colleagues and battle buddies is also an excellent way to mitigate your leadership cocoon. I reached out to several long-term friends and brought them into positions where they could use their incredible talents for Canada and the Canadian Forces, and in doing so put them in easy reach for frank discussions when issues were troubling me. Peter Atkinson, who became the fifth Canadian general to fill the appointment of deputy commanding general at Fort Hood since Joyce and I went there in 1998, was my special assistant. He was the link between me and my key staff in Ottawa when we were away and became a sounding board for me on every topic you could imagine. Since he was with me everywhere, it probably wore on him more than me. Walt Natynczyk, as both Chief of Transformation and then Vice Chief of the Defence Staff before replacing me as Chief, was my sounding board on every issue. I knew both men well and trusted them implicitly. Ron Buck, predecessor to Walt as Vice Chief, was a refreshingly honest man who could get to the root of a problem and help me solve it in a nanosecond. Bill Brough, long-time friend and colleague, became my special assistant during the preparation for the mission in Afghanistan and its execution. He, along with people like Rita LePage, Serge Labbe, US Brigadier-General Les Fuller and George Petrolekus, became part of my support group and, through our unified strength, enabled us to accomplish significant things.

British Prime Minister Benjamin Disraeli once said that he thought he knew the weight of the responsibility of office when he took it, but it was really apparent only when he handed back the keys to No. 10 Downing Street. There is much truth to this. No matter what you do, the responsibility that you as a leader carry will set you apart from those you lead. You will find it from time to time a little lonely to be the boss, and sometimes a lot lonely. Do what you can to help others help you. Build personal teams, no matter whether they work directly for you or not, learn whom to trust and then use those teams and individuals and their trusted advice, personal counsel or clear views of an issue, no matter where in the world you and they may be.

BEING DECISIVE MEANS PISSING PEOPLE OFF

When you make a decision, someone will always be unhappy, possibly even royally pissed. You can minimize the damage that comes from this, but you can't mitigate it completely. You simply have to deal with it. The more responsibility you have as a leader, the more serious the decisions you will be called upon to make and the more serious the implications of those decisions.

About a year after becoming Chief of the Defence Staff, I started to realize that I would get to make few good, and easy, decisions. We had done a pretty good job articulating our vision and putting leaders in place to implement that vision, and we had government support and the support of Canadians to achieve the vision. This meant that all the real operational decisions would be made by commanders in specific regions or on external missions, and those were the decisions that had to be the right ones. It also meant that easy decisions, where all were in agreement, were also made long before I would be called upon. This was good. It also meant that the only decisions I had to make were the really tough ones. Any decision the Chief of the Defence Staff makes will please someone and piss someone else off. There's no way around it. You will never have enough money, people or time to do everything, and therefore some people will be angry.

Perhaps one situation that was really sensitive for me was the future of Canadian Forces Base (CFB) Goose Bay, in Labrador, in my home province. Fighting to balance never-ending demands with limited resources, I had to reduce the wastage in administration and overhead, specifically by closing infrastructure, in the form of bases, that no longer served any operational purpose. I felt that tasks formerly done at the base were now all being done elsewhere, yet we had millions of dollars and more than a hundred people tied up there without purpose. It was a politically sensitive issue. My birth province deemed it had far too small a percentage of the defence dollars spent in Canada, the people in the area depended on Goose Bay for jobs, members of the Senate and Parliament were up in arms and I was vilified on radio talk shows in Newfoundland and demonized in conference calls by ministers from the provincial government. It didn't faze me though. My job was to maximize the operational capability in the Canadian Forces for Canada and that did not include excess infrastructure. Jobs, percentage of federal dollars and political sensitivity were not my responsibility and, as I explained numerous times, one excess base took away a fighting ship's crew; the money it took to keep that base in existence meant we would not have the ship either.

My point is that any decisions I made were bound to anger someone. In this case, if I ignored the excess infrastructure, I'd be criticized for not getting enough ships, planes and troops operationally ready. And if I pushed for closures? Well, what happened in Newfoundland was a good indicator. In my last week as Chief of the Defence Staff, I had discussion with Minister of National Defence Peter MacKay on the subject of CFB Goose Bay. I remained firm: "The Canadian Forces has no further operational use for it, and if it stays, someone else should pay. If jobs are the driving factor, put Coast Guard ships in, entice a business to start up or do something else. Of course, that's my opinion as Chief of the Defence Staff. Next week, when I'm no longer chief and become the chancellor of Memorial University in Newfoundland, my opinion will change. CFB Goose Bay will be essential to saving the free world!"

Know that your decisions will anger some while pleasing others. This cannot keep you from making decisions—that, after all, is your job as a leader—but knowing what will occur can enable you to mitigate some of the irritation.

CHAPTER 45

You Are Not Alone: Seek Strength

Every leader has to realize that he or she will have dark days. The shape of the darkness will be dramatically different from one profession to another. It can mean financial collapse, infrastructure failure, personal attacks or allegations about you, or it can be scandal involving those you trust. I found no days darker than those when we received word of the loss of life among the men and women who wore the uniform. Whether it was the day a Snowbird pilot was killed when his plane crashed during a rehearsal for an air show, the day a search and rescue crew was killed when their Cormorant helicopter plunged into the dark and cold Atlantic off Nova Scotia in the middle of a training exercise or the days our soldiers were killed in Afghanistan by the Taliban, those days have been indelibly marked in my memory.

During the darkest of days, people will almost always withdraw into themselves. I have never fully understood, from a psychological standpoint, why this is, though I have had it explained to me thoroughly. But it is true. And withdrawing into yourself can be disastrous, especially for leaders. It's during the darkest days when people most need to be inspired and comforted. They need to believe there are brighter days ahead, and you as the leader need to step up and help bring that hope. When things go badly, don't seclude yourself in the office, cancel appointments, sit hunched over the desk, head in hands, in the late-afternoon gloom—get back out there. Withdrawing is dangerous. It leads to people jumping off forty-storey buildings or ending their lives in other equally tragic ways. You need to reach out and find inspiration yourself, and then use that inspiration to inspire and lead others. You will be astounded by the results.

I desperately needed inspiration when my troops died. Few individuals can carry the weight of the most tragic events by themselves, and most of those who can are not the kinds of human beings you would want as leaders. So I'm not admitting to weakness here; rather, I'm facing up to the facts. I had to be inspired to continue myself during those tough days.

The source of my inspiration surprised me. I was motivated by ordinary Canadians who cared. They had been moved by the efforts of our wounded soldiers, by their resilience, dedication and courage. Canadians from coast to coast responded so powerfully to them, to the rest of us in uniform and in support of the families that it was inspiring to all. Most surprisingly, I found myself inspired by the families of the soldiers who had been killed, people I thought would need inspiration themselves.

The Canadians who inspired me came from all walks of life. They emailed, phoned, wrote to me and talked to me in person when I most needed it. Some grabbed my hand and were too choked up to speak. Others spoke eloquently. Some cried on my shoulder, and I shed tears with many. The Warren family, who had lost a son in Afghanistan, also had a daughter in the service and they, in their pride and grief, encouraged me to recruit their only other son. The Dinning family, after losing their son Matt, a military policeman, on 22 April 2006, asked my help in removing obstacles so their other son could also become the military policeman he wanted to be. The Dallaire family, Gaetan and Diane, who had lost their son Kevin on 3 August 2006, participated in every event involving our soldiers and families that they could and arranged for Canadian Blood Services to have more than twenty thousand Christmas cards for our deployed troops signed by Canadians. Gaetan continued to give blood—almost two hundred donations—plus numerous plasma donations. If, as the Canadian Blood Services says, one donation saves or dramatically improves the lives of three to four people, Gaetan has helped to save hundreds of Canadians. It seemed that at every event that sent a chill down my spine—a Red Rally to support the troops, a Run in Red, a Military Families Fund gala ball or dinner in Calgary—I could turn around and see the Dallaires. They are incredible (but, sadly, continue to denigrate the Toronto Maple Leafs).

I went to Trenton to meet every family waiting to receive the body of a son or daughter, husband or wife, father or mother, brother or sister. The intention of the senior leaders of the CF was to support them through the worst days of their lives, starting from when we first got off the plane in Trenton to meet them. We shed tears with these families. We told them just how proud we were of their soldiers, their loved ones. We also laughed at stories of the soldiers' exploits, the trouble they had gotten in to when younger, the escapades escaped and the dreams finally realized. And we talked about their love for soldiering. Before we knew it, we were the ones being inspired by the strength, courage, love and humour of the families, whose characteristics had so clearly been reflected in our soldiers who had been killed. We left Trenton inspired and recommitted to what we had to do as leaders.

I also had a small personal team that helped keep me going. Honourable and incredible people like Major Iain Huddleston, my aide, whose common sense and people skills were put to constant use to keep me on course. Two men in the appointment of the senior serviceman in the Canadian Forces, Chief Warrant Officer Danny Gilbert, with his extroverted good humour and commonsense approach to life, and later Chief Warrant Officer Greg Lacroix, with his balanced view and gravitas, along with their wives, helped to keep me going.

There were others, from across all parts of Canadian society. I met two seemingly very ordinary Canadians whose compassion made them extraordinary and whose presence will stay with me forever: Michel and Don Gardiner, who distinguished themselves from the crowd first through the mail and then personally at a Red Rally in Bridgewater, Nova Scotia, in May 2008. They had written a poem, a copy of which I keep with me and reread frequently. It inspires me to this day:

You Are Not Alone

When you rise in the morning and face the day
You are not alone

When you're out on patrol and in harm's way

You are not alone

When the goals of the mission seem impossible to keep
You are not alone

When you lie still at night and can't fall asleep
You are not alone

We are with you, supporting you, praying for you
We are standing by you in our hearts
We are loyal to you in our words

You are a reason I can proudly say

I AM CANADIAN

There were thousands of others. You, as a leader facing difficult and stressful times, have to seek and find your own sources of strength. Men like Kevin Reed, a businessman who instigated Project Hero, where universities and colleges across Canada sponsor the children of our fallen through to bachelor-degree education, and Gerry Nudds who raised money for many causes, including—and touching my heart especially—the teddy bears with digital recorders for the children of deploying soldiers so they could leave messages to be listened to while away.

Remember as you go about your business as a leader that you are only human. You are susceptible to the pressures of the job and you can break. Reach out to your circles of colleagues and friends and to family to find the inspiration and the strength you need.

TRUST YOUR BATTLE BUDDIES

The last thing you need to worry about when dedicating every waking hour to meeting your responsibilities is whether you can trust someone. There are always backstabbing ladder climbers who failed the ethics test but carried on anyway. One of the most powerful ways to help determine who you can trust, to build a bond that gives you confidence when times are tough, is accomplishing tough tasks as a team. Once you have done that, you can be comfortable that someone has got your back. You can then start to widen your circle of trust. You simply don't have to worry about people with whom you've literally, or figuratively, been under fire. These are the people we in the military call "battle buddies." No person is more trusted than the one who's been with you under fire in battle. You can rely on a battle buddy for life.

You can build your own team of trusted battle buddies. I'm not advocating that you get your friends together and have someone shoot at you—of course not! But it's very difficult to hire only those people you trust, unless you hire only those you know well, and we know from past scandals that this does not always work out well. To build trust, you need to share training and operational experiences. And you need to remember that trust goes both ways, from you to the team and from the team to you.

I relied on battle buddies like Walt Natynczyk, now Chief of the Defence Staff. I soldiered with Walt for twenty-five years. He became my deputy, as the Vice Chief of the Defence Staff; before that he was key in driving the transformation of the Canadian Forces. I discussed every issue with him, knowing that he would give me frank and objective advice that would remain between us. I trusted him implicitly, and when he said I needed to pay attention to something, I did. There were also the people who had become battle buddies through recent training and operations— the military police who made up my small, close protection team.

These military policemen—professional, capable, dedicated and personable—were with Joyce and me constantly. We quickly gained confidence in them and learned that we could trust them completely. And we had to: our very lives were in their hands. When we travelled internationally, the need for close protection we knew and trusted became an issue because most countries want to provide such protection themselves. I got a wake-up call on one visit, after which I insisted that at least one of my team accompany me at all times. My experiences taught me all about trusting one's battle buddies and how important it can be.

I had complete faith in the team members, from how they behaved to how they did their job and cared for and handled their weapons. Many times in foreign countries, surrounded by people I did not know who were armed to the teeth, I felt that I was more at risk from them, and accidents, than any prepared attack. This was confirmed for me when I visited one South American country that insisted on providing close protection. Usually such protection means an outer ring of people, a "box" directly around me and always a personal protection officer right next to me. I assented and, on arrival, met the personal protection officer, who stuck to me like Velcro. He was constantly close but, unfortunately, he was not invisible, a skill my team had perfected.

After freshening up following the long trip from Canada, I went to a cocktail reception in the hotel ballroom. About two hundred people were in attendance. Trying to mingle and meet as many of the other guests as possible, I would find myself a part of a small circle of eight to ten people, then, after a short while, I would move on to another circle, with my personal protection officer at my left side. In was while in one of these small circles that I was shocked by an explosion—the detonation of several small arm rounds next to me. My ears rang, and I could smell burning cloth. The others stood stunned as plaster dust fell on me from the ceiling, where the bullets had hit.

My erstwhile protector had had his machine pistol in the waistband of his pants. It had slipped down his right pant leg, the butt of the weapon striking the floor, and fired several rounds, which came through the outside of his pant leg—hence the smell of burning material. The rounds then travelled upward between him and me and hit the ceiling. I still had a ringing in my ear when we left two days later. I had lost faith in the protection of armed personnel I did not know and whose background I could not assess. My battle buddies always went with me after that, and I never permitted anyone around me with a weapon unless I knew and trusted them.

You might not have had such a signal experience, with bullets whizzing past your ear, to convince you to trust a core group, but take it from me: build a list of battle buddies you trust implicitly, even with your life.

FITNESS COUNTS

One of the great preparatory steps you can take to help ensure your success as a leader, particularly to enable you to weather long and difficult days, monstrous amounts of travel, broken hours and pressure to always get it right is to ensure that you are physically fit and then stay that way. You have to find a type of exercise that works for you and that you find enjoyable. If you're not having fun, the exercise will become drudgery and can even add additional stress, and likely you won't stay with it. So whether golf, running or wheelchair basketball is your thing, keep doing it to keep your body fit. As a young officer, I came to believe that a healthy body leads to a healthy mind, and I still believe this to be true.

The benefits are many. First, doing any fitness activity will ensure a break from endless routine—be it meetings, study or preparations where muscles become stiff, blood flow is interrupted and the brain is not properly supplied with oxygen to help you think. If you aren't exercising and reducing stress, you're setting yourself up for a heart attack sooner or later. Throw in an unhealthy diet, add a few cigars after special events (my personal weakness) and the occasional overindulgence in alcohol and you are setting yourself up for failure. You may be fortunate enough to have a harmless indicator that tells you its time to change your lifestyle, but not everybody is as lucky. I'm not talking about living the life of a warrior monk but about a simple, common-sense approach based on where you are: the particular stage of life you are in and what you are doing.

As a soldier, I was fortunate to belong to a profession that held fitness to be next to godliness. I was also fortunate that I enjoyed it immensely. I loved running, even with combat boots and a rucksack on. That probably led to one of the stupidest things I've ever done: the Special Service Force Ironman competition. I think I did it because I loved the pain, not because I was particularly well prepared for it. My running had been limited following a severe ankle break during a parachuting accident, so my preparation had not included the distance or weight needed to truly be ready. The competition was a marathon done in combat uniform, with boots, carrying a rucksack with thirty-five pounds of kit and an automatic weapon. On completion of the initial 36-kilometre run, the weight of a canoe, two paddles and a life jacket were added as each participant portaged his or her canoe four kilometres. This was immediately followed by a ten-kilometre canoe paddle and a final four-kilometre run with just rucksack and weapon. I was fit, but this was exercise at a new level and I knew it would be tough.

Early in the morning about 115 of us launched. As a lieutenant-colonel, I was easily the oldest and most senior in rank.

The first part was not easy but played to my strength: an ability to keep running like an Energizer bunny. The portage almost finished me, however, because I had not rigged my canoe well and instead of being able to carry it easily over my head on the frame of my rucksack, I had to keep holding it up with my arms, no easy task in the gusting winds that lifted it off my body. I was getting dehydrated by this time, and the competition was becoming gruelling. Joyce, who was there at this particular point to cheer me on, figured I was a goner and wondered how she was going to break the news to the family. I got through the portage, but by the time I hit the water and started canoeing, the wind had picked up even more and was pushing me constantly onto shore. The two paddles, which I had secured together like a kayak paddle, now served me terribly, since I constantly had to push off from just the one side, the other paddle sticking way up in the air. When I finally did get to the finish point and tried to get out of the canoe, my legs refused to cooperate, cramping extensively. I pretty much had to be held up in the air until my legs dropped down. The last four kilometres were easy after that.

Being fairly stubborn, I went home to take a bath after this seven-hour exhaustive effort, figuring to go back to the Officers' Mess for a cold beer. The first indication that I was perhaps not ready to do much for the next few hours was my scream when the hot water hit the two large abrasions on my lower back. Rubbing from the rucksack had worn the skin away in two large spots. Persevering, I got myself cleaned up, then went to the mess for a beer, where I finally had to admit to myself that I was tired and headed back home. The small coin I earned from the commander for my efforts seemed insignificant then but is prized now. Even more amusing than thinking about that day is listening to my son, who completed the same competition just two years ago and tells similar stories. We Hillier men never learn.

I also really enjoyed swimming, scuba diving and golfing. In fact, I tried my hand at pretty much every sport or recreational activity there is, including hockey (a sport which I see as our national "religion"), which I played at every opportunity, though not well. As a leader in combat units for years, "presence is important" meant that I was expected to be on morning physical fitness training with my troops, so there was no excuse or reason to not be. There is no better way to start a day than a great workout like a morning run along the Ottawa River with three or four thousand of my battle buddies. If I started out lacking energy and had to push myself just to get out of bed, within ten minutes of being with Canada's sons and daughters, I was really fired up.

Perhaps the most memorable run I was on was at Fort Hood, Texas. The corps commander set up a corps run of about eight kilometres to celebrate the 225th birthday of the US Army. Thirty-six thousand troops, divided into their many units, each with their pennants and all of them chanting marching songs, took part in the run. The commander led from the starting point, which was also close to the finish line. I followed with the staff, and the units fell in based on seniority. The route was marked by 1st Cavalry Division troopers in their traditional western cavalry uniform, on their horses. Their band played at the starting line, and the 4th Infantry Division Band marked the turning point. The women who worked at the largest grocery store in the area stayed up all night to bake and decorate an enormous birthday cake, about eight feet by eight feet. There were so many people running that when the commander and I finished, the last units still had not even started the race.

The workout made us fitter, but its team-building aspect was even more valuable. Perhaps even more valuable still was the feeling that all the participants had, and which lasted for at least the next six weeks. That feeling was one of cameraderie, being part of a team, realizing we were all working to achieve our mission and having pride in wearing our uniforms. It was inspiring to see all the parts of the enormous team come together, and it was something to remember.

When I was brigade commander in Petawawa, we in the brigade managed to combine the fitness need with the team-building and communications aspects in almost everything we did. We held brigade events every six weeks or so. We started a rucksack march just after I took command and when most units had all their soldiers back from summer leave. I led the brigade headquarters staff from our building. Wearing our battle kit and rucksacks, we marched around the base, picking up the various units at their unit headquarters as we went. We then headed out to the training area to complete a good workout, about four thousand of us together, and returned to one of the parade squares on base. We became fit and built an awareness of and appreciation for the bigger team.

When we returned to the parade square, we formed up on three sides of a square and I had all the troops sit on their rucksacks. I then was able to talk directly to everyone, from the senior leaders to those who carried bayonets on the front line. We all had one message, one view, of where we were going, what we were going to achieve, how we were going to do that and what part each one of us had to play. Every six weeks we did this kind of event, whether it was a ten-kilometre run or a snowshoe march in our white, winter camouflage. Each event allowed me to achieve most of the leadership impact I've talked about in this book, while keeping me fit.

The most positive and lasting effect from such events carried me through tough times. But I also remember having clearer thoughts about various issues during those workouts than I had at any other time. My mind was clear. I ran in a dissociative manner, that is, without thinking about running, so I could think about other things. Often when I finished I had resolved conflicting priorities and had come to conclusions and made decisions that I had been putting off.

Runs also broke up my day. Long days in National Defence Headquarters in Ottawa could break even the strongest man or woman, and a run, somewhere near the middle of the day, was just what the doctor ordered to restore me. I even ran in winter; once I ran up the frozen Rideau Canal when it was minus forty-five degrees Celsius with the wind chill, and I felt great.

The day I announced my retirement, a large number of people were endeavouring to contact me, and since I wanted to talk to none of them right then, I went for a run. I was chased down Sparks Street in Ottawa by a reporter in a tight skirt and high-heel shoes, asking me questions and trying to dig out her recorder as she attempted to run alongside me.

Any kind of workout gave my brain a rush of oxygenated blood to counter the stale air from the conference rooms that at times were the bane of my existence. When I start my day with any kind of exercise, the day goes better. No matter how cold it was on winter days in Petawawa, after being outside for just fifteen minutes—warming up first and then running, skiing or snowshoeing—the cold weather felt tolerable. After a shower I would often go out the door without even putting my coat on. Without such a workout, the day felt colder, I was more prone to hide where it was warm and certainly I was not as productive.

During the fifteen or twenty minutes I spent in the gym cooling down after my exercise, I had a chance to meet and talk to people whose tracks I was unlikely to cross if I hadn't gone for a workout. I learned what was going on, how things were being done and how people felt about everything, which was all important. It kept me more situationally aware than anything did—except smoking! There was nothing quite so informative as huddling outside in the smoking area listening to smokers from all different levels and branches of my organization. Funny how both ends of the health spectrum offered the most value for that.

Lastly, put together a small group to motivate you and to make you feel guilty if you don't get out. Fitness is important, and it can literally mean the difference between life and death for you. Start now.

CHAPTER 48

HUMOUR SAVES

One of the very best tools that a leader has, both to relieve stress and to build the morale, cohesion and shared experiences a group needs, is humour. Perhaps it is my Newfoundland heritage, but humour has always been a part of my life. Cracking a joke, laughing at myself or laughing with someone else seemed to lighten my load, made me feel less cold during winter exercise, reduced the pain of long hours, alleviated the stress of intense work and simply made it fun to go to work each day and be a soldier. Humour made me feel better, and I'm convinced it made others cope better too. What we remember from past experiences is how we felt at the time, and humour helps to mark those experiences in our memory in the most positive way.

Humour seemed such a normal and powerful tool to me that I made it a part of everything I did, and pointed out to all and sundry the value of it. When building the International Security Assistance Force (ISAF) leadership team to command the mission to Afghanistan in early 2004, we, the senior leaders, were faced with the Herculean task of building a functional command group supported by a staff team that not only would not lose ground during our time in the theatre of operations but actually could advance the cause of peace and stability significantly. On top of that, we had to be prepared for the worst-case scenarios from the very first day on the job in Kabul. (After all, we would have no say as to when terrorists might attack.) We were challenged by our disparate group: thirty-seven nations contributing troops to the headquarters, numerous language problems, sometimes conflicting cultures (for example, former Warsaw Pact officers working inside NATO structures), interference from national capitals and simply the fact that none of us knew the others. We had just two weeks to get ready and were being assessed by a NATO team from about day three of our preparation. At that point I had not even met everyone attending the training.

Clearly, we had our work cut out for us, but it went well, and even though we faced personality conflicts, had difficulty understanding each other and experienced other stressors besides the operational kind, we ended up laughing a lot. I started each day detailing what we were doing, how we needed to approach our effort and what each of us was required to contribute. I made it a bit more detailed and challenging each day but always found something to elicit a laugh. Usually there were sufficient stories about pitfalls from the previous day, things that I had gotten wrong or related stories I could tell that were funny and still made key points. My drawings (I complemented my words with sketches) usually were a cause for laughter too. People were in good spirits, learning and developing visibly on an hourly basis.

The last several days of the two-week training was occupied by a mission rehearsal exercise, run by the aforementioned NATO assessors, who put us through a full workout that simulated being on the mission in Kabul. When we started this specific part of the training, I took the opportunity to lay out my approach—how I believed we needed to work together—in what I referred to as my nine rules. Most of those rules were specific to the ISAF mission and precisely what we would be doing but the last, Rule Nine, was to use humour at every appropriate opportunity to relieve stress, lighten the load and have fun. It caught on.

Humour was an important part of how we handled the challenges we faced, a key part of the way we built our cohesive team and an important part of keeping the stress bearable. During every event, meeting or after-action review, someone would crack a joke or request permission (or beg forgiveness afterward) to tell a short story. Rule Nine became a part of who we were as the ISAF team, followed us into theatre and still, six years after that exercise in Germany continues to link us around the globe. I immediately open emails from my friends that have as a subject line, "Rule Nine."

Humour breaks the tension, keeps things from appearing weightier than they are and is a powerful team-building exercise. Sometimes I saw examples of gallows humour, and there's nothing wrong with that. Gallows humour communicates a feeling, and the greatest danger for people is that in times of stress they won't communicate their feelings.

One young soldier on the mission to Kandahar in 2008 perhaps carried gallows humour to the extreme. Knowing the power of the improvised explosive devices used by the Taliban, he had each of his arms and legs tattooed with the same instruction: "Return to sender."

Humour is powerful and one of the best tools available for your team, and also for you personally. When you can smile, the keys of office do not seem so heavy.

313

CHAPTER 49

LOOK AFTER YOURSELF

You have failed as a leader if, at the critical moment when you and your leadership can make a difference for all those who are inspired by you, who have confidence in you and who work hard for you, you collapse, freeze or depart and cannot do your job. If the crisis that causes your departure is health, mental or physical, and it was something that you could have prevented by basic commonsense, understanding and a few consistent actions, your failure would be criminal.

You are a human being and therefore imperfect, with strong points and vulnerabilities and both strengths and weaknesses as a leader. The effect of these characteristics and skills is magnified by the demands of being in a leadership role, obviously more if you are a leader with enormous responsibility and accountability. If you are not careful about taking care of yourself, you can fail. Look after yourself is the message because unless you do so, you cannot look after those who follow you.

Be at the top of your game because you have taken steps to put, and keep, yourself there.

WHEN ALL ELSE FAILS

When you are in trouble, the world is falling in around your ears, your reputation is being shredded, stress is high, friends are few, bosses are angry and complete failure looms, go back to Rule One: Focus on People. You can't go far wrong.

Good luck.

ACKNOWLEDGEMENTS

As with *A Soldier First*, this book would not have seen the light of day without the help of many: my family, whose patience has been tried but found to be unending; Chris Wattie, who again helped turn my words into something resembling the English language; John Pearce; and Jim Gifford and his entire team at HarperCollins who, with patience and professionalism, helped guide all the pieces into place. Thanks to them, and to the many others whose stories I got to share.

ACKNOWLEDGMENTS